Ben Canaider was **not** born in India in 1946. Following this he did **not** attend Oxford University in any capacity, a time he now does **not** have mixed feelings about. In the late 1960s he was **not** a confidant of John Lennon nor did he experiment with psychotropic drugs. As a result of this he did **not** lead a Bicycle Freedom Rally through the southern states of the USA, which did **not** lead to his appointment and ultimately his much-publicised sacking from the chair of Women's Studies at the University of Copacabana. This experience was then in **no way** the basis of the first novel Mr Canaider did **not** write (based loosely on the early life of Barry Manilow), titled *But Who Shot Who?* He does **not** live in Massachusetts with either a wife or a partner – or a Labrador. He does **not** meditate on Buddha as a way of dealing with his non-existent inner demons, he is **not** a former winner of the Whitbread Prize, and he does **not** collect works by experimental watercolourists of the inter-war years.

In a dreary and dipsomaniacal reality, **Ben Canaider** types about drinking for glossy magazines and newspaper lift-outs. This is his second grown-up book.

Also by Ben Canaider

Drink Drank Drunk
Beer: Slabs, Stubbies and Six-packs
Cooking Under the Influence
The Perfect Glass of Wine

HOW TO DRINK ABSOLUTELY EVERYTHING

BEN CANAIDER

RANDOM HOUSE AUSTRALIA

Random House Australia Pty Ltd
Level 3, 100 Pacific Highway, North Sydney NSW 2060
www.randomhouse.com.au

Sydney   New York   Toronto
London   Auckland   Johannesburg

First published by Random House Australia 2007

National Library of Australia
Cataloguing-in-Publication Entry

   Canaider, Ben.
   How to drink absolutely everything.

   ISBN 978 1 74166 465 2 (pbk.).

   1. Canaider, Ben – Travel. 2. Drinking of alcoholic
   beverages. 3. Drinking behavior. I. Title.

   641.2023

Typeset in 12/16 pt Palatino by Midland Typesetters, Australia
Printed and bound by Griffin Press, South Australia

10 9 8 7 6 5 4 3 2 1

Contents

This book is dedicated to Theodor Seuss Geisel,
who so wisely advised in his *Sleep Book*:

'. . . when goose gets a mouthful of juices of moose's
And moose gets a mouthful of juices of goose's,
They always fall out of their beds screaming screams.
SO . . .
I'm warning you, now! Never drink in your dreams.'

And don't mix your drinks. Thank you, Dr Seuss.

Introduction

What follows these introductory remarks is an account of the mostly forgotten and invariably ill-gotten life of a professional drinker. Drinking is what I do to survive. I get paid to drink. Most of this work is for glossy magazines and those food and wine lift-outs in the newspapers. Posh people describe me as a 'wine writer', but I prefer to think of myself more as a typist who drinks. Part of the job involves tasting a lot of wine – about 3000 bottles a year. Then there are the beer, spirits and liqueurs. Yes, I'm omnibibulous. But I don't necessarily enjoy them all. About 90 per cent of what I drink is awful. The remaining 10 per cent not only stands out and gives me something to write about, but it also lifts my inebriated spirits. From Aardvark Liqueur to Zubrowka, I wade through alcohol for a living, desperately trying to keep my head above water, trusting in some tipsy fate that a mastery over the liquid dominion will keep me clothed and fed – otherwise people might take me for a drunk and not an expert.

That being said, most of the time I stagger and slump somewhere between those two evil extremes. There's a loose process and a determined spontaneity. Sometimes I drink when I should be thinking and at other times I think when I should be well and truly on the juice. Discipline is not entirely disregarded, however.

In order to bring as much professionalism to my job as I can, I try to break the working day up into snack breaks. Rather than the daily three-square beverages, I like to graze: Breakfast; Morning Tea; Instant Lift-Off; Luncheon; Port; Afternoon Tea; The Cocktail Hour (or Beer O'Clock); Pre-Dinner Drinks; Dinner; Dessert; Après Dinner; One Million O'Clock; The Wee Small Hours . . . There's a drink to go with every one of these occasions. A 10 am Bloody Mary; an 11 am glass of sherry; a pre-luncheon Martini; whites wines and lighter red wines at luncheon; a small vintage port to settle the afternoon down a little; a Campari and soda to bring me up to Cocktail Hour speed; a gin and tonic with too much lime; a beer in the pub to stimulate an appetite for dinner, which will need to be harmonised with a few glasses of various wines; a short glass of muscat with the pudding; a single malt whisky with the late-night news, before failing to retire to bed and finding that mojitos at one million o'clock in a bar with no name full of fifteen-minute friends are all too healthfully refreshing.

In this way every day is an education. I am ever-curious and always eager to acquire new information. Perhaps this is because I find it so hard to remember? Or do people drink to forget? Maybe those old men sleeping rough and wandering the streets know the answer to that question. For the moment, all I can do is warn you about the inherent dangers found in the pages to come. Yet in their irresponsibility the responsible service of alcohol might shine. Each and every day, a glass of wine, a beer after work, a nightcap or a heart-starter. Inch by inch rather than binge by binge. In other words, in moderation. Yeah, good luck with that.

1

Without hangovers there might not be the Bloody Mary . . .

Eat bitter almonds and drink half a glass of cauliflower juice diluted by fresh water and wear a necklace with an amethyst pendant.
– a hangover cure from *The Fragrance of Basil* by Raffaela Delmonte

This story starts on a bean bag. Two bean bags, in fact. They contained two young boys. The boys and the bean bags were plopped in front of an old black and white television set with one of those bakelite and steel remote controls connected to it via a long electrical cord. You pressed one of the buttons on the control and about three and a half seconds later the television channel-changer would grind around a couple of stops to the next station. Sometimes it would go one station too far, and you'd have to throw the remote into reverse and try to land it back on the right channel. This could be more fun than actually watching the television show itself.

1

Along with the bean bags and the two adolescent boys was a bottle of old red wine. That perhaps needs some explaining. Or maybe not. This is a book about drinking, after all.

I'd requisitioned the wine from my father's very small and very humble collection of old reds. It was a bottle of 1968 Wynns Ovens Valley Burgundy. We had no idea who this Wynns person was, nor where the Ovens Valley lay. We thought Ovens might have been the explorer. Burgundy was a similar mystery. But let's move on. Talk of wine is invariably boring.

My friend Bradley had asked me if I'd ever had a drink. I didn't understand what he meant at first. When you are fifteen your mind is not automatically defaulting to alcohol at every given question or occasion. It was as if he'd asked me if I'd ever breathed in air. But then the penny dropped and I realised he was talking about grog. Or *the drink*, as my mother called it.

'Nnnner, of course . . .' I replied, telling a lie. 'We drink wine.'

'Have you got any we could drink now?' he continued.

'Yeah.'

Thus was my transition from innocent sobriety to naïve alcoholic dependence; it was as simple and as straightforward as that.

I lithely rose from my caramel-coloured corduroy bean bag and made for the wine cupboard. I don't remember how I opened the bottle, but opened it was, with me and Bradley and two milk glasses on said bean bags in front of the old black and white television with the remote control on the end of the long electrical cable. It was a Wednesday night and Mum and Dad were out doing one of their second jobs. Bradley and I were on the bean bags watching *The Goodies* or *Doctor Who* followed by an English cops and robbers show called *The Professionals* or an English cops and robbers show called *The Sweeney*. Television was all very British back then. At some stage during the evening the wine ran out. Bradley went to pour himself another glass and the bottle was empty.

'Jeez!' he said, in what we both imagined to be an entirely sober tone of voice. 'Why do people reckon that wine makes you drunk? That's easy to drink!'

In the manner of one who has from that evening on shown no hesitation in moving from one bottle to the next, I decided to do the hospitable thing and dig out another red. Rising once more from the bean bag, I promptly fell flat on my face. As soon as I'd stood up all my muscles had turned to jelly, and in what seemed like most of an eternity my strangely detached mind plummeted to earth. My head was buried in the piebald woollen carpet of the back room of the house, and Bradley was rolling out of his bean bag in a fit of drunken laughter. That's where the evening's recollection ends. And where my drinking career started. I have no regrets. At least, not now. The next day at school sports was a different story.

We lived and went to school on the top of a small mountain. The athletics ground upon which we annually played out the tragedies of school sports was at the foot of the mountain, on the flats. The bus took us down and around the mountain at a pace and movement that was unhelpful to anyone suffering from their very first hangover. Not that I knew I had a hangover at the time. I thought I was suffering from travel sickness. The Phys Ed teacher looked at me sitting half out of my bus seat, trying to breathe while trying not to throw up, and asked if I was

OK. I looked up at her and she nearly shrieked. 'Oh, Ben, hang on, we are nearly there. You are almost *green* . . .'

Bradley was greener than green. He was so sick that he couldn't even sit next to me or talk to me or look at me. But he did have the additional burden of carrying the evidence. Thinking that we'd be in trouble if Mum and Dad found the empty bottle, Bradley had put it in his school bag, figuring we would dump it once we left home. He hadn't managed to yet. It was still in his bag, under the bus seat.

Not being terribly interested in team sports I had not enrolled in any event. For such a crime I'd been given two detention sessions. They were very interesting lunchtimes. Bradley was going through a bit of a read-stories-about-ancient-Greece phase, so he was keen on something called the javelin. In the middle of an athletics ground in which the majority of forms two, three and four were besporting themselves, Bradley launched the javelin. In the wrong direction. It cleared the running track and landed, pinpoint, right next to a bin on a grassy knoll near the perimeter fence.

We pulled the javelin out of the ground and lay on the knoll for the rest of the afternoon in the rough wind and patchy sunshine of an early spring day. We ate bags of chips and drank cola from the sporting ground's tuck shop. This made us feel much better – fats and sugars. Bradley put the rubbish in the bin. When the day ended and we were lining up to board the bus, I saw our History teacher walking the perimeter fence checking for lost clothes, bags and – with less interest or concern – children. He walked past the bin on our grassy knoll. He stopped. He did a bit of a double-take on the bin. He put his hand into the bin and pulled out an empty bottle of

Wynns Ovens Valley Burgundy, 1968. He was clearly struggling to suspend disbelief. And that was the first time I ever laughed as a result of alcohol. No wonder I love my job.

Or was it hard-wired into me? Does alcoholism run in families? Did I have a genetic predisposition towards drinking? I've been wondering about this for some time now. It's like I'm trying to find an answer to why I drink and why I am so good at drinking. Really. I could drink for Australia. I could be a gold-medal winner. Rocky Balboa lamented that he didn't get a chance to be a con-tender. My problem is that my sport has no organised competition. Maybe that's why I like it. Thinking of Rocky and thinking of boxing, I naturally started to think about the brain. Maybe the answer to my drinking lay inside it. First things first, though; I had to locate it.

The Canaider family brain has been with us for a while now. I think my great grandfather did the last upgrade, back in the 1880s. Needless to say, they don't make Italian machinery like that any more. You can tell it is an Italian brain because the on/off switch is upside down. There's also a little light on the front that glows during the brain's warm-up period. It's just like a panini machine – when the light goes out the machine is ready to use. So I got it out, dusted it off, turned it on. Nothing happened. Turned it off and then turned it on again. Something rattled inside and then the light glowed. Fifteen minutes later I could safely and confidently use it; and I used it to try to understand why this brain seemed to only run on alcohol.

Brain waves, neurotransmitters and serotonin function, protein production and the brain's central amygdala. Hypertension and a hyperactive central nervous system, missing neuropeptide receptors, skeletons in a chromosome number two's cupboard ... There's a raft of scary science to suggest that your penchant for putting a few away was there the very second you came into being. With the right breeding you can be predisposed towards drinking and alcoholism. Predisposed; not predestined. Like homosexuality or vegetarianism, your genes play about a 50 per cent role in the potential or the end result. And not all of us with such a drunken ghost in the machine are going to turn into antisocial alcoholics. We become non-antisocial alcoholics. The difference between the two might have something to do with Dylan Thomas's definition of the general condition: 'An alcoholic is someone you don't like who drinks as much as you do.' The trouble is, I don't know anyone who drinks as much as I do. I wonder if Dylan and I would have got along OK?

Brain waves and the central nervous system are one area of the ever-distilling research into alcoholism's hard-wiring. A brain-wave spike occurs a zillionth of a second after you've noticed some sort of sensory surprise. Say, the flash of an annoying camera. Alcoholics and people predisposed towards alcoholism experience a much smaller brain-wave spike than the sober side of humanity. The theory is that this low spike indicates that your central nervous system is relatively uninhibited. You've got an excitable brain. Alcohol calms it down; but then dependence kicks in and you need more and more of the drug to do the job.

Neurotransmitters and serotonin also play a weird role. Messages flying around our brains somehow interact with alcohol molecules, which in turn increase our appetite for the drug. Neurotransmitters associated with stress levels and traumatic reactions go haywire when we don't get our glass of wine at luncheon. Do I keep drinking in order to defeat this genetically pre-programmed tendency towards anxiety and tension? Or am I a heavily evolved *Homo sapiens*, the sophisticated product of thousands of years of alcohol's cohabitation with man?

However, that doesn't explain the presence of so-called anti-drink genes in some members of humanity. If you are of Asian decent then there is a fair chance you are going to possess one. It is borne out by facial flushing. People whose face and ears flush visibly upon taking a drink probably have this anti-drink gene. Ingest some alcohol and blood rushes to your face. This happens because of the first step in alcohol breakdown – our bodies turn alcohol into acetaldehyde. This stuff is also responsible for the rapid movement of blood. Acetaldehyde is broken down into acetate by an enzyme called aldehyde dehydrogenase. People who suffer from facial flushing have a slower-acting version of this enzyme, hence the build-up of acetaldehyde – and the quicker and more severe onset of hangover. On a medical research level, it is hard to understand how people so afflicted (or are they lucky?) can drink at all. But they do. If one in two Asians have this anti-drink gene then why are rates of alcoholism so similar in Japan, China and Korea compared to such bastions of immoderate freedom as the US and Canada? Piercing your ear hurts, but people still do it. Mountain climbers die, but people still keep climbing mountains. Maybe it is not so specific, this whole alcoholism-in-the-family deal. Maybe general craziness is the issue. That is certainly the case with a member of my immediate family – Charlie. He had crazy and drunken turns. But he was a cockatoo.

And he was a cockatoo that liked whisky. And toothpaste, too; so he couldn't have been all bad. He was also deeply devoted to our mother, but didn't much care for our dad; which was an inverse alignment of affection when compared to all the other siblings.

Charlie just couldn't help himself where whisky was concerned. Ninety per cent of the time he was a normal sulphur-crested cockatoo, resting on his perch in the lounge room, flying around the bedrooms, or walking up and down the hallway like a white-feathered version of Charlie Chaplin, his gait all side-to-side and cock-a-hoop. He was well-versed, as many cockatoos tend to be. Among his favourite utterances were 'Peeeeete!', which was the endearing way in which my mother would yell at our father. Then there was 'Lurch! Lurch! Stop it, Lurch!' which was the endearing way our father would yell at the pet Weimaraner when it was pulling the side off the sofa. Charlie also quite liked yelling out 'The keys! The keys!' whenever my older brother would try to 'borrow' my mother's Volkswagen; and he was fairly keen on third-person self-reference: 'Charlie! Charlie! Charlie!' But sometimes he would yell out 'Monty! Monty! Monty!' which was my brother Mark's family name. This was odd because he would often do this when Mark wasn't home; and he would invariably yell this out just before he had, as my Uncle Mick used to call it, *one of his attacks* . . .

It didn't matter where the whisky bottle was hidden or locked up, Charlie would get to it. Doors would come off cupboards, lids off big preserving jars. He would rip out the cork stopper with his powerful and desperate beak and knock the bottle to the floor, dropping his head side-on to the ground, his little grey parrot tongue licking up the whisky from the very corner of his fully-extended beak. His wings would start to spread out wide and his crest would rise and fall in violent motion. Speech gave way to wild screeching, and if you got too close to him he would fix you with a frightening, cold, blurry one-eyed stare, like some crazed berserk warrior about to slit the throat of an imagined enemy. He would fall about and walk in circles. And he would then use the bathroom.

Drunks, of course, often find various guises of refuge in bathrooms. Maybe Charlie wanted to be alone. Maybe it was shame. I don't think so. I used to run to the neighbours and hide under their kitchen table when Charlie took to the bathroom. Because that's what he did. He would *take to it* with every ounce of his beak and talons' strength. Taps ran, mirrors were smashed, bathroom shelves removed from walls, light fittings ripped from ceilings and dashed on the floor. And when it was all over, Charlie would be sitting in the corner, amid the piles of wreckage and the flooding water, holding a tube of toothpaste in one foot, sucking on the end of it with his beaky mouth. He was like a baby with a bottle. My uncle used to wonder if he was concerned about being caught with the smell of whisky on his breath . . .

Mum saw the wry side of it too. Not.

'No, Mick, he gets it from his father; he gets it from Pete. We all know how he goes when he drinks . . .'

And he did drink, my dad, on a few occasions to spectacular effect. It sent me, once again, running to hide. To my bedroom. Under the blankets. Sometimes under the bed. But then Dad stopped the hard stuff and I reckon I didn't see anyone drunk again for ten years, until my older brother came to visit one day on his motorcycle. I was standing in the driveway and Mark ran over my foot on a 850 cc Moto Guzzi. When he did stop the bike nearly fell over; and he nearly fell over trying to take his helmet off. My mother came outside and desperately and sadly uttered, 'Oh, Monty . . .'

Mark recovered, as did my foot. But it was shortly after this incident that I found myself falling over too. Falling over a bean bag. Which brings me to the topic of my present job, or role. And it brings me to a particular Saturday-night-cum-Sunday-morning when things had got a little out of hand and I'd got a little bit sideways. Personal recovery might very well have been impossible, but for the fact that God in His wisdom had invented two very necessary things: the Bloody Mary and the Elvis impersonator. They saved me.

When Saturday night becomes Sunday morning you can experience a terrible flash of unkind reality. It occurs at that moment when the never-ending notion of the night becomes the unavoidable truth of the next day. It is the drinker's version of mortality. You realise the good times will end. It can get you at 9.30 pm. You can get it at 5 am. You can get it any old how.

Sometimes this realisation is but a glimpse, like a shadow falling and disappearing. Sometimes it is the full technicolor projection of the horrors of your drunken ways. It hits you like a high-velocity brick; the illusion of happiness is shattered. You then want Sunday to come quick, so that the debacle you've made of Saturday can be forgiven by Sunday's (surely) more worthwhile and honest endeavours. Sunday morning can be a strange time for retrospective and disjointed, reverse chronological thinking. Bits and pieces of the immediate past come back in to what is left of your tiny mind.

It had all started on Saturday afternoon. Actually, on Friday night. Well, let's make it Friday. At lunch. The food service at one of my favourite business facilities was slow, which meant I drank faster than I ate. I should've known better, but at the time, what with some light, sunny weather and some reasonable business company, I didn't stop to think; I just kept up the liquid pace. Friday lunch became Friday after-work drinks became Friday night out on it with some other non-friends who had some reason or other to be celebrating (I can't recall just what the reason was). Friday became Saturday and Saturday lunch was very necessary because I was feeling a bit tired and so the whole thing continued anew and afresh and with an obvious yet entirely unseen J-curve crescendo.

The girlfriend of the time also chose Saturday at about 4.30 pm to tell me it was over. It was a bit of a shock, because everything had been going swimmingly and I'd thought she was the one. She got a bit teary and I pretended to take it well and she left via the front door muttering one of those chick-lit Mills & Boon sorts of lines about how she *loved me but was not in love with me* . . . I went straight to the pub, ringing a mate, and we drank pink gins and mojitos and that's where I ran into a girl who was a regular and who was always very friendly and she bought me another drink when I told her no, things were not going really well with, oh, for the sake of the story let's call her Gwendolyn, as we had just broken up. The early evening was ticking along nicely and the party of about five had by now decided that pizza would be in order. That's when Gwendolyn rang and said she was sorry and that maybe if we just took things a bit more slowly for a while, and could I still join her and her friends for dinner that night. Of course.

The friendly regular's reaction to the news that I would be unavailable for pizza I do not recall, probably because I left the pub immediately and went to shave and shower and change for dinner. And buy a bottle of champagne. I must have been quite pissed by that stage because the champagne somehow sort of went everywhere when I opened it at the dinner party and I vaguely remember some of Gwendolyn's friends being a bit embarrassed by something or other and I vividly recall Gwendolyn yelling at me in the hallway and then I remember being asked to *Ben-just-go* and getting back to the pub and managing to run into the friendly regular and having dinner that I think was just her and me and then ending up back at my place after pushing the friendly regular there in a supermarket trolley. I came to at about 6 am and the only part of the friendly regular still present was an earring. I sat up in bed, naked and alone, thinking that this was how I would be for the rest of my life. Having drunk so much, the levels of maudlin in my toxic body were high, and feeling pathetic and full of self-pity I turned to the only person who could save me.

Schopenhauer.

It was what Schopenhauer had said about emotional helplessness and love's loss that I tried to cling on to. He'd advised that no matter how low you felt about your emotional predicament, you should take some sort of comfort in the fact that you were not the first person to ever feel this way in the history of mankind, nor would you be the last. Others have survived and been happy once more, so there was no reason why you couldn't do that too. So I decided to get out and about in the world again. Immediately. I went to the Sunday-morning junk market. It was a kind of home-away-from-home anyway. But I wasn't out of the hangover woods just yet.

Sunday morning's quiet and calm unease had created this odd vacuum inside my head. Maybe even in my body. My entire spirit. I started to think this was a deep yearning for the loss of something very ritualistic and otherworldly in my being. Hundreds of years of Sunday-morning churchgoing had left an imprint on my dusty DNA, and now – without that churchgoing – I felt a little bit lost. This must have led me to junk markets in the first place. Junk markets are full of lost people.

Empty Sunday-morning roads were the first step in the surreal and hung-over journey. In a trip that was at all other times underscored by traffic-laden, angst-ridden gear-grinding, this Sunday-morning jaunt was eerie. The roads were mostly empty. You didn't have to use the brakes. The car seemed to float to the market. Given that hands and eyes and feet and legs were all cotton wool, that was probably a good thing. Reaction times were not just slowed, they were in another time–space dimension. Yet that is forgiven. Junk markets need hung-over people. Hung-over people do not look for bargains at a junk market; bargains find them. All a hung-over person needs to do is buy an egg and bacon roll and, as long as it is still before 8 am, eat it while watching the Elvis impersonator – a bloke, coincidentally enough, called Elvis.

By now I'd started to spastically recall some of the more specific moments from the previous night's highlights reel. We'd drunk bottles of Spanish red wine over dinner at a bar in a Spanish-style tapas joint. And we'd kicked off the dinner with sherry. I had drunk that aperitif like beer. So I wasn't only feeling sick-hung-over; I was also more than a little discombobulated. Having bought the e&b roll I headed through the car-park junk market, past stalls of old clothes, bric-a-brac, crafts, potted plants, dodgy militaria, unvaluable china and porcelain figurines. I made it to the western edge of the car park just as Elvis was setting up. We were coming into spring and he was clearly going to turn it on. This week he was wearing the fully-sick sequin suit complete with built-in half-cape. Elvis's raggedy and poorly barbered sideburns seemed a little more carefully cut, too. He'd recently washed his hair, and it was mostly in place. The nervous and possibly medically related twitch and agitated shaking of his left hand was absent. The only thing that remained odd was the choice of footwear. Ugg boots. Dirty, over-size Ugg boots. Beggars can't be choosers.

Elvis was a tall and lanky man. He'd been Elvis ever since I could remember. This spring was my twenty-third at this market, and my fuzzy mind figured him around for mostly all of that time. Sometimes he would go away for a while. Not to the Gold Coast (he wasn't a crim). Not for a holiday (he didn't have money, so he didn't have money problems . . .). He went to stay with 'family', as one stallholder had told me. He'd stay with family. In a hospital. For a few weeks. His family all wore white coats and knew the psychiatric drug secrets. They cared for him more than they loved him, and they gave him tablets and helped him to sleep. For days and nights. But did he dream? Perhaps he did, and then he would come back into the world and be Elvis again, with a new suit of clothes and new cut of hair and a new pair of somebody else's over-size shoes. In the middle of those twenty-three years, when I'd run a stall at this market, I'd always asked for a spot near Elvis's unconsecrated stage. Some stallholders didn't like Elvis's routine; in his early days he'd perform all around the market, moving from one spot to another, picking up tiny amounts of loose change in what passed for his busker's cap as he did so. He never made much because people were scared of him. Because he was free and – as Elvis – uninhibited. Once he started the performance the Dionysian switch would be thrown and he was away. The nervous chaos that was his off-stage presence would vanish. This made him frightening, I guess. Lots of people would walk past his show and not even look; they did that comfortable suburban look-the-other-way thing, pretending that the junk stalls to their left were real and the Elvis impersonator shouting and dancing and prancing to their right did not fucking well exist at all.

For four years I had that stall near Elvis. Occasionally, when I was feeling pathetic or superior or just plain out of it I'd buy him an egg and bacon roll. He'd take the roll; he'd never look at me. And without a drip of irony or humour he'd always say *Thank-you-very-much* . . . He could look pretty rough some days; on others he'd not be able to get his voice beyond an occasional whimper.

Some performances would go for a few minutes, with him frantically starting and stopping and fast-forwarding and rewinding through the tracks on his tape player; other shows seemed seamlessly choreographed and perfectly built, with ballads, love songs, anthems, gospel and extended R&B numbers rolled out just at the right moment.

This Elvis impersonator was a little different, it needs to be said. Elvis held a microphone with about five feet of cord hanging off the end of it, connected to nothing. The cassette deck sat on the ground near his busker's cap. The cassette deck played a tape of Elvis's (the real Elvis's) live performances. *The Impossible Dream*, *Always on My Mind*, *For the Good Times*, *You Gave Me a Mountain*, *It's Impossible*, *It's Over* . . .

Elvis (the impersonator) would stand behind the cassette deck and hit the play button and, holding the microphone, would start doing Elvis moves. With no connection to the music or singing or (real) Elvis comments coming out of the cassette deck, Elvis (the impersonator) would talk and occasionally sing along to the tape. It was as if Elvis (the real Elvis) had a twin brother who was a few ingredients short of a full hamburger, and that twin brother was on stage, somewhere in the dark background, singing along with his famous brother, adding his own comments to the live performance; kicking in with some supporting vocals every now and then. In this sense this Elvis impersonator was the most humble of them all. And people wouldn't look at him. I don't get that. But I was hung over and feeling old. And my body was like cotton wool. And I was being entertained by a strangely detached Elvis impersonator in a suburban junk market at 7.53 am on the last Sunday before the vernal equinox, thinking that maybe this was my sick yearning for and strange version of a church service. (The gospel numbers always got to me.) Schopenhauer's sentiment was failing to keep me mentally upright. Elvis's gospels were unravelling me again. Alcohol levels were beginning to drop dangerously low. A Virgin Mary wouldn't do; I needed a Bloody Mary to help me re-embrace humanity at the start of a new week, and to bring hope back to millions of my brain cells.

There is a look you get whenever you order a Bloody Mary. It is a look that contains an entirely understandable but nevertheless regrettable, silent rhetorical question: 'You're hung over, aren't you?' That one of the 1920s' greatest and most versatile cocktails should generate such a thought pattern is a little sad. The Bloody Mary is not merely a hangover cure, it is a drink in its own right; it is the breakfast you have moments before you order lunch; and it is the vitamin supplement that younger detoxers otherwise call a 'juice'. It is a gazpacho soup acting as your first course; and it is a wonderful way to eat celery sticks. More of us, therefore, need to stand up and defend the nobility of this wonderful drink – a drink that might contain anything up to seven different types of alcohol, or none at all. Yes, yes, that is a Virgin Mary, and it's on my rabbinical list of banned dietary substances, but you get my drift . . . More importantly, the Bloody Mary should never be treated or considered in a pejorative way. For without hangovers there might not be the Bloody Mary. And the world of drinking would be the poorer for it.

Yet we don't only have hangovers to thank for the creation of this drink. The Bloody Mary came from Harry's New York Bar in Paris, in or around 1920. Of course it did. And the drink was the culmination of a strange set of events. A jockey in New York State was winning a lot of races, but also betting on his own horses. He got caught so he had to leave New York. The jockey had a friend who owned a bar. Together they moved to Paris and set up another bar called Clancy's. They employed a Scotsman called Harry to run it; and he eventually ended up owning the whole joint. Hence Harry's Bar. Harry subsequently hired the mixologist of the day, a bloke called Pete Petiot. He was the first man to mix tomato juice and vodka, and the theory goes that he only did it because he was trying to find some way to make vodka more mainstream. Vodka had only recently arrived following the Russian revolution. Post-1917 Russian émigrés brought the drink with them, mostly to Paris. But if you reckon an age-old Russian ingredient made the Bloody Mary possible, well, that's only half the story. Tinned tomato juice – an early twentieth-century American invention – completed the equation. And that's what I love about this story: the way we make a Bloody Mary now is exactly the way they made it 85 years ago.

Although that depends upon the recipe you subscribe to. And there are a lot. The Bloody Maria is an Italian take on things, substituting grappa for the vodka. It is the sort of drink that should come with a prescription. The Wasabi Mary swaps horseradish (an optional ingredient in the standard Bloody) for wasabi; it's got some soy sauce as well, rather than Worcestershire sauce. Another rather interesting take on Bloody events is the Sting Ray. In this Bloody the straight tomato juice is replaced with clamato juice. Yes, tomato juice and ocean clam juice. Blue Crab Bay Company 'Sting Ray' Bloody Mary mixer, from Vancouver, is what I've been applying to myself of late – very late in the morning. It's more salty than fishy, which is probably a good thing, and in a big-enough glass it is almost an entrée in its own right. Speaking of which, you could always whiz yourself up a Macho Gazpacho. Instead of using tomato, juice up some Spanish onion, red and green peppers, cucumber, celery, and a jalapeno chilli. Pour it over the ice and vodka and hello world.

Heat is another common sidestep in the Bloody Mary shuffle. Chilli-infused vodka is every second barman's secret weapon. Muddled fresh horseradish provides something akin to an olfactory-oscopy. It certainly gets your frontal lobe moving. Most bars opt for the stuff in the jars; however, this pre-loved horseradish gives you the trace of flavour, but not the kick. Cayenne pepper is probably the most potent ingredient, particularly if used in incorrect proportions. Anything more than a knife-point of this stuff is dangerous. Cayenne is also one of the original ingredients in the very first Bloody Mary. Over ice it was mixed in with the vodka, tomato juice, lemon juice, Worcestershire sauce, and salt. That was it: the classic Bloody Mary. Nowadays we see more cayenne used for rimming. A glass's rim is rubbed with lemon juice before being dipped into a saucer containing a fine layer of cayenne. Given that most Bloodies come with a straw, and that's the way they are consumed, the cayenne doesn't get to play the active role it once did. An alternative and more exotic twist on rimming and on flavour additives can be found in Middle-Eastern-flavoured Bloodies (yes, a bit of an oxymoron . . .). In its modern Middle-Eastern guise, North African and Levantine spices go on and in the glass. It gives the Bloody a coarser texture and, depending on your attitude, the spices are either flavour boosts or speed humps on the road to recovery.

A more common way to get heat into the drink nowadays is via hot pepper sauces, like Tabasco. The red pepper sauce, made from Tabasco chillies, is the standard, although there's a green pepper sauce version for a bit more cut and thrust.

Of course, a Bloody wouldn't be a Bloody if it didn't have a secret ingredient. But in this case it is not so much a secret one as an overlooked ingredient. Lemon juice. A squeezed quarter of a lemon doesn't do it; you need more than that. The only thing that makes a Bloody Mary stand up and sing is the simplest and most healthful ingredient of the lot. Go long on the lemon juice and lunch will come neatly and quickly into focus. Depending on the hangover . . .

There are, apparently, somewhere between six and nine types of hangover; but I have this only on authority. Being a professional drinker I only ever tend to get one type of hangover – a really, really bad one that borders on toxic shock syndrome – and then only very, very occasionally. If I did get the full range of hangovers as advertised, regardless of how much or how little I had drunk, then I'd be an amateur. The tax deductions would then probably not stand.

Given that drunkenness has been drunkenness ever since Adam was a naughty boy, hangovers probably haven't changed much over the centuries, although what with modern food and beverage standards we perhaps nowadays do not ingest the sorts of toxins and poisons once found in our drinks. The ancient Greeks, given the mood and the sort of party they found themselves at, were not averse to a cup of wine flavoured with some lead. (And some post-modern wine lovers find it hard to accept screw-caps?)

Your hangover probably depends on your initial type of drunkenness, however; although there never seems to be any water-tight rhyme or reason to this. A few *woines* at a *noice* dinner party and you can wake up on Saturday morning feeling like shit; yet get giddy at three different pubs with a group of friends and the next day you might be more inclined to eat some yum cha than you normally are, but otherwise you're functioning OK. You can even sign cheques.

The man who knew something about these variations on the drunken theme was Thomas Nashe, a late-sixteenth-century English dramatist and satirist. He was a man compared latterly to James Joyce. Extraordinary vigour and energy went into Nashe's pamphlets. He started out by writing a pamphlet called *The Anatomy of Absurdity*. It put a few of the toffs off. Nashe wasn't afraid to relax with a beverage after work, nor did he mind hanging around with other Elizabethan trouble-makers, like Robert Greene and Ben Johnson (both solid drinkers. Pisspots. No wonder the only work they could get was playwriting). Thus alcoholically inspired, Nashe's satiric and vituperative plays often took on the sorts of powerful people that, so mocked, led to Nashe spending a bit of time in the Fleet prison. He died at the age of thirty-four. But he had already lived a little, particularly when you consider that at the age of only twenty-five he'd composed a pamphlet called *Pierce Penniless his Supplication to the Devil*. It contained Nashe's drunken menagerie, or the eight different kinds of drunkenness.

The first is Ape drunk, which *leapes and sings and hollowes*; the second is Lion drunk, *and he flings the pots about the house, calls his Hostesse Whore, breaks the glass windowes with his dagger, and is apt to quarrell with any man that speaks to him* (in other words, this bloke is a footballer); the third is *Swine drunke, heavy, lumpish and sleepie, and cries for a little more drinke*; fourth is *Sheepe drunke, wise in his own conceit, when he cannot bring forth a right word*; fifth is a form of drunkenness that we have all either witnessed or experienced, *Mawdlen drunke, when a fellow will weepe for kindness in the middle of his Ale, and kise you saying 'By God, Captaine, I love thee, goe thy waies, thou dost not think so often of me as I do of thee. I would (if it pleased God) could I not love thee so well as I do', and then he puts his finger in his ere, and cries*. Yep, that's a shocker. Sixth is the state I'm mostly in – *Martin drunke, when a man is drunke and drinkes himself sober ere he stirre*. (That's harder to do than you might imagine, and takes some training.) Seventh is *Goate drunke, when in his drunkenness he hath no mind but on lechery* – thank goodness I have never suffered from that form of the condition . . . And finally the eighth type: *Foxe drunke, when he is craftie drunke, as many of the Dutch men bee who will never bargaine but when they are drunke*.

Interestingly, Nashe wrote this pamphlet while staying at the house of one Archbishop Whitgift, in Croydon, just south – and now a part – of greater London. Recent accounts of alcohol-related civic disturbances in the area probably differ little from what Nashe might have seen – and been involved in – over 400 years ago. He was a bit of a Martin drunke, though – the state I most relate to.

The condition is named for Saint Martin of Tours, the Patron Saint of Drunkards. He wasn't always on it, but his name was used for Martinmas, and Saint Martinmas Day, on 11 November. (Earlier, this date had been the Roman Vinalia, or Feast of Bacchus.) The eleventh – before climate change, at least – was the last hooray for the English, in terms of the metrological year. It was a time typified by some late, summery weather. An Indian summer, as the Americans call it. There was a fair bit of celebrating and social drinking at around the time of Saint Martinmas Day, when you might drink for a few days at a time. I understand that entirely. For me each day is not, as Frank Sinatra sang, Valentine's Day, but more like 11 November. But that is the unromantic reality of my job, and of having to drink to pay the bills.

Drunkenness and its categorisation only gets us so far, however. It is the hangover that concerns health-addicts like me to a much greater extent. Which is why you need to consult an appropriate doctor, like P. G. Wodehouse did. Wodehouse thought there were six hangovers: the Atomic, the Broken Compass, the Cement Mixer, the Comet, the Gremlin Boogie, and the Sewing Machine. No doubt Bertie Wooster suffered each and every one of them at some time or other in his brilliant Peter Pan-ish career; yet they mattered only for a short while, thanks to Jeeves's restorative elixir. Bertie would send it down the hatch with all the courage the code of the Woosters could muster, and – BANG – he'd be adjusting the collar of his heliotrope pyjamas before manfully tucking into his eggs and b. Perhaps Jeeves's cure was based on a Bloody Mary?

Whatever, it was the eggs and bacon immediately thereafter that no doubt helped. Indeed, recent Australian research suggests the Aussie breakfast classic – Vegemite toast – is about as close as you can get to a perfect, restorative return to solids. Carbohydrate in the form of the toast and lots of salt and Vitamin B in the form of the Vegemite. But there are more theories about hangover cures than there are scientific and sociological explanations of how we get them.

The only real cure for a hangover is death. But that might be taking things a little too far.

2

The imperfect Martini

The Zen Martini: A martini with no vermouth at all.
And no gin, either.
– P. J. O'Rourke

Thoughts of hangover or drunkenness or of poor genes, well, none of these thoughts ever seem to be too close to mind or heart when one is within easy hand's reach of a Martini. Like champagne, the Martini has for some strange reason a very profound effect on anyone about to meet it. As the American historian and critic Bernard De Voto put it so perfectly: 'You can no more keep a Martini in the refrigerator than you can keep a kiss there. The proper union of gin and vermouth is a great and sudden glory; it is one of the happiest marriages on earth and one of the shortest-lived.'

Fleeting perfection is the Martini's talent, and its curse. The cocktail's innate simplicity adds to both conditions. This is why you need the very best examples of the Martini's two ingredients to be getting anywhere close to the mark. And then there's the way you make it; and the glass it is served in; and the person you are with (if in company . . .); and the person you are yourself. Some personalities do not understand this wonderful cocktail; it seems to grate against them. Or they grate against the Martini. Yet along with chardonnay, cola, and decaf soy latte, it is arguably one of the most influential and most swallowed drinks of the last century – so it is odd that we should so often get the Martini so wrong. With this drink, imperfection is always but a small shoe-size shuffle away. Given the cocktail's genealogy, it is no wonder.

An American gold prospector and the Churchills are to thank – or to blame, whichever way your attitude to this drink goes. To understand this ancestry we need to adopt a mode of thinking more commonly found in the Old Testament, in Genesis. It involves the wonderful word 'begat'.

First of all (and before any of that begetting stuff), let's get one thing straight: the Martini is *the* cocktail. It has written more novels and inspired more actors and disempowered more leading ladies than you could shake a cocktail mixer at. From James Bond to Philip Larkin, it is a drink that has had a hold – being used either as a weapon of conquest or a tool of self-captivating self-destruction. And all it takes is not much gin and even less vermouth. Stories about the Martini's origins and invention abound with more vigour than a Thomson's Gazelle on cocaine – or its third Martini – but the most straightforward and believable line of antecedence follows the evolutionary development of two earlier drinks.

The Martini itself started to take hold in the US (and then very quickly in England) at the turn of the twentieth century. At its inception a Martini was about one-to-one gin and vermouth. (Something hardcore Martini drinkers will find hard to come at one hundred or so years later.) Vermouth's contribution dropped to a third of the mix during World War I, and to a quarter by World War II. One could speculate that the drink was quickly improving thanks to the general degustatory evolution of the human race – we evolved and we liked dryer drinks. Yet I can't help but think that two world wars might have something to do with it. Gin, after all, is about as twice as powerful as vermouth. So why stick to the weak stuff? As Leo Tolstoy uttered in a suitably *fin de siècle* off-note, circa 1891, people drink 'not merely for want of something better to do to while away their time, or to raise the spirits, not because of the pleasure they receive, but simply and solely in order to drown the warning voice of conscience.' It is a wonder, therefore, that by 1939 there was any vermouth left in the Martini at all.

The Martini started its evolutionary trail as the Martinez; the Martinez begat the Manhattan; and the Manhattan begat the Martini. That's where the begetting of the breed stopped. Since the Martini we've had no more evolutionary worth. Dirty Martinis are self-explanatory. Whisky Martinis are a waste of two good spirits. Chocolate Martinis need to be immediately and irrefragably cast from all thought. Begetting became a belated belabouring. But let's get back to the goldminer and the Churchills.

Winston Churchill's American mom, Lady Randolph Churchill, held a drinks party for New York's new Governor in 1874. Lady Churchill was then some months away from meeting Lord Churchill; she was but a nineteen-year-old socialite with a rich daddy and an ambitious mother. The bash was at the Manhattan Club and Lady Churchill (aka Miss Jennie Jerome) wanted an original mixed drink for the occasion. The bartender of the grand old joint, in the spacious private lounge behind the limestone, neo-classical façade of 56th Street, stirred rye whisky, sweet vermouth, and a dash of angostura bitters together in a glass. He popped a maraschino cherry on top and dutifully named the concoction the *Manhattan*. The vermouth helped the medicine go down and the bitters heightened the flavour of the whole show. The rye was the medicine and the maraschino cherry the poison.

Let me explain. Nowadays, of course, maraschino cherries are extraordinarily healthful, but back in the nineteenth century such sugar-syrup-flavoured cherries were often dyed, in order to set a consistent colour. The trouble was, the dye was toxic. Another Manhattan, Lady Churchill? No wonder the party went off.

So the Manhattan is the Martini's father. The rye whisky represents a bit of old America, I suppose. Daddy might be called a Manhattan, but there's a bit of a fist-fight in him yet, frontier or Pocahontas style – or whichever way you like. Otherwise the family resemblance comes out in both the father's and the son's inherent simplicity. A sharp spirit soothed by a fortified, aromatised wine called vermouth. The simplicity explains why both are two of America's favourite cocktails, and two of the 50 or so classic cocktails informally recognised by the New York Bartenders' Union.

Yet before these two generations we find a slightly more boisterous member of the family, which some think came from out west. The Martinez is no more and no less than a Manhattan made with gin, albeit a sweetened English gin by the name of Old Tom. No, just Old Tom.

There is no 'Cat' at the end of that name. The theory is that a Californian goldminer hit it big in a Californian town called Martinez, back in the 1850s. Celebrating at the Occidental Hotel in San Francisco, the miner had the legendary barman Professor Jerry Thomas fix him a special drink. He painted the town beige that night, and so was born a mixed drink – named after the goldmining town forty miles to the east. Dry vermouth, gin (Old Tom), maraschino cherry liqueur, angostura bitters and a twist of lemon zest. Oh, and a maraschino cherry, just to be sure. It was the immediate ancestor of the Manhattan, and suited to the more ebullient tastes of a goldminer newly flushed with the wherewithal. Just how the Martini was begot by this Martinez creature is another thing.

And it has something to do with the ever evolving nature of taste. Children like sweet things; adults like dry or bitter things. Apparently when we end up at about sixty-nine-and-a-half years old we all go back to liking sweet flavours again. It has something to do with the way we taste. Tip of tongue equals sweet; back of mouth equals bitter. Ripe fruit was sweet and safe; poisonous fruit was bitter and deathly. As this is true of general human development, so it is true of any particular culture's development. Mixed drinks based on spirits during America's nineteenth century evolved into the early twentieth century's cocktails. Generation change happened at each and every level, and, as a result, cocktails became dryer and clearer. Hence the Martinez became the Martini.

The precise genealogical line is a tricky one. As close as any sort of research can show is that an Italian barman at New York's Knickerbocker Hotel – a man called Martini di Arma di Taggia – was mixing such a drink so named in 1910. At this time Martinis were also being made with sweet red Italian vermouth. How quickly things changed. And it got to the point where a true Martini aficionado would only ever pass a bottle of stoppered vermouth over the top of the gin-filled shaker ... That, according to the son of the woman responsible for so much of the whole thing, was the essence of a great Martini. Then again, Winston did like to start the day with a whisky and soda in bed, as he read ministerial papers. War was hell, but mornings in bed were real R&R.

Anyone who hasn't bothered with either a Martinez or a Manhattan shouldn't, by law, be allowed to drink a Martini. It's like cheating at golf, or copying someone else's homework. You've got to do the right thing by the family and have a few cocktails with Dad and Granddad before you get out on the tear with the young Mr Martini. But in what state should you find him? How should he be dressed? Where should you go? And what of the conversation?

There is a physical and metaphysical element to every Martini. Mixing them at home, you need to understand – and execute to the letter – the former. The physical elements are all-important. When out with a Martini, however, it is critical you are in silent tune with the meta-physical nature of this drink. And if you don't believe this then you have failed to come to grips with the fact that each and every single Martini is a much better person than you can ever hope to be. It is a blindingly spectacular, sudden and searingly brief shaken (or stirred) supernova.

The physical Martini requires two ingredients – and the right approach. To start with, it helps if you own your own home. Smug people make better Martinis than non-homeowners. I do not know why this is, but it is. Cruel, but true. Non-homeowners shouldn't be put off making a Martini at home, however; and if, after your third one, you accidentally drop the Martini glass and tread the broken shards of glass into the polished floorboards, well, it's not your place really anyway, so no need to care.

Before any of the equipment or ingredients are mentioned it is also very important to be in the right frame of mind. You need a carefree, relaxed approach. You need to go about making a Martini as if there is not a problem in the world – at least not a problem affecting you. Which is why I always pretend, just before mixing a Martini, that I've won the lottery. And bought a house. If you are worrying over that dumb thing at work or why the car has a weird noise in the motor when you haven't got the stereo up loud enough or how you are going to get out of the family barbecue next Sunday lunchtime, well, the Martini is not going to like your lack of full and fond attention. Martinis are egoists; they are very self-centred drinks, living life as if the world revolves around them. This is why all Martinis, no matter what time of year they are made, well and truly fall under the astrological sign Aries. So, be relaxed as you go about the procedure. Don't be too much of a hippy, but don't be one of the cocktail scientists measuring everything down to the last nanosecond, molecule, and degree Kelvin. Love your Martini, and it will love you.

First: keep your Martini glass in the freezer. If you've got ice cream in there, or frozen peas, or a frozen chicken or stock or any food – chuck it all out. Freezers are for

Martini glasses and ice. And vodka. But not gin – I'll explain this bit in a minute. As for other equipment and materials, you'll need some ice cubes, a cocktail shaker with a fine strainer and the two liquid ingredients – gin and vermouth.

Use Noilly Prat French vermouth, otherwise known as dry vermouth. Not much of it, of course. Keep this in the fridge; once opened it is fairly bullet-proof fortified wine, but it will lose some of its aromatics after three months or so. Keeping it in the fridge slows the aromatic loss down.

I mentioned that vermouth is a fortified wine – and it is a fortified wine that is about as far away from *wine* as you can get. It's mostly made like white wine, then it is aged for a little while, then it has grape spirit added. Thus fortified, the wine is put in barrels to which all the aromatics and botanicals that make vermouth *vermouth* have been placed: cinnamon, quinine, orange and lemon peel, cloves, ginger, and – in the good old days – some wormwood. (Wormwood was the key psychotropic in absinthe.) The word vermouth itself comes from the old German word for wormwood, *wermuth*; but vermouth has a history that morphs back in time to the Ancient Greeks, who regularly put herbs in wine – as much to hide off and spoiled flavours as anything else. Vermouth took off as a curative or medicinal drink during the sixteenth century. It was highly regarded as a sore tummy cure, and two areas of vermouth production saw two distinct styles of the drink come about. Around Piedmont in north-west Italy, and close to the Alps where the various botanicals could be found, came sweet vermouth made from red wine. Over the border, on the other side of the Alps, dry vermouth was being made, mostly from white wine. This pale vermouth was also slightly bitter. So French is usually dry vermouth and Italian vermouth is red and sweet. Or white and sweet. In fact, all styles of vermouth are now made in both countries. There's even vermouth made in the United States, but no one I know would drink that. Cinzano Bianco is the world's best-known brand; it's a sweet vermouth. Carpano's Punt e Mes is an Italian red vermouth that is quite viscous, combining both sweet and dry vermouth in a single expression of the style. This sort of stuff is not to be laughed at – but treated with some respect. Over in Bordeaux, another type of pale/golden vermouth is made with the addition of fruit juices – it goes by the name Lillet. Dubonnet is one more French version, with more quinine in the mix, and lower alcohol, at about 15 per cent. But this is all incidental to our cause: a classic Martini needs dry French vermouth, Noilly Prat, from Marseillan – a little town on the edge of the Etang de Thau, two-thirds of the way between Montpellier and Béziers. So nowhere near the Alps at all . . .

Of course, there are plenty of hardcore Martini-inspired, self-regarding wits and raconteurs who sophisticatedly believe that the ideal amount of vermouth in a perfect Martini is none at all. Advising anyone silly enough to be paying them any attention, they comment: *Simply pass the stopper over the top of the gin as it sits in the Martini glass . . .* The dangerous romance of this practice is a little bit dulled nowadays anyway. We have screw-cap lids on bottles of vermouth in the twenty-first century, and being theatrical with a screw-cap is hardly the derring-do of a cork-stopper conjurer.

Besides, using no vermouth in a Martini might see the humble yet no less worshipful bottle of vermouth disappear, as it nearly did a hundred or so years ago. Without the creation of the Martini, would vermouth still be with us today?

Like a lot of time-honoured and vaguely medicinal drinks, vermouth had come a bit unstuck by the time the twentieth century had come around. Patent medicinal powders and liquids were receiving more marketing and salesmanship than latter-day anti-aging creams. Potions relying on traditional and largely natural ingredients and properties (such things as cinnamon and wormwood and alcohol) were seen as a bit antiquated and old hat. Moreover, they didn't have the punching power of some of the new wonder elixirs: morphine, cocaine, heroin and Coca-Cola. And the old-fashioned herbs and roots weren't nearly as addictive as these new coca and opium derivatives either.

Opium had been around since the seventeenth century, and everyone who was anyone was on the stuff. Samuel Taylor Coleridge took it for a toothache and then wrote *Kubla Kahn*. Sir Walter Scott was feeling generally off-colour and resorted to opium. The result was *The Bride of Lammermoor*. Wilkie Collins medicated his rheumatism and depression about his sick mother with the Big O and then pumped out *The Moonstone*. (And if you've ever had any doubt that *The Moonstone* isn't a drug book . . .) Charles Dickens used opium to help him get through a book-reading tour in the United States (fair enough, too) and then went a bit funny in *The Mystery of Edwin Drood*. Even Florence Nightingale was on opium – for a sore back. The story would be even better if, in this state, she was inspired to head off to the Crimea. Unfortunately not. She was back from the war and milling around London, something of a celebrity. Not the Kate

Moss of her day, perhaps, but then no one knew she was on the gear . . .

Of course, the thing is that such drugs were not considered bad back then. They were the Panadol of their day. They did wonderful things for sick people – who then became addicted to them and proceeded to do horrible things to non-sick people in order to stay on the supply line. Nothing has changed in this last respect.

And the drug kept taking new forms. Opium begat morphine in 1803. Another offspring was codeine. Scientists of the day were now on a roll, discovering all sorts of essential components in the plant world that had strong mental and physical effects on human beings: like quinine, caffeine and nicotine. And then, just before 1860, someone was clever enough to put the coca plant under the microscope. Ladies and gentlemen, all be upstanding (all night) for cocaine . . .

Believing that the essence of the coca plant was both an elixir to man and also a profit centre for himself, a chemist called Angelo Mariani invented a health wine in 1863 called Vin Mariani. Queen Victoria drank this stuff, a glass just after dinner. The Pope was on it, too. So popular did Vin Mariani become that copies of it sprang up all over the place, including in the US. In Atlanta during the 1870s, a drug-maker called John Pemberton produced a drink called French Wine Coca. Pemberton was a morphine addict, but otherwise ran a successful small business, like a lot of drug dealers do, one must suppose. There was a crude theory among drug-makers at the time (which might have been Pemberton's real interest in the plant extract) that coca's cocaine could possibly alleviate and then cure an addiction to opium and morphine. (Not true, we know now; but a search for a hot turkey substitute for these addictive drugs continued, one such creation being, in 1898, heroin. It was another opium descendant, and at the time of its release was thought to be non-addictive.)

Pemberton was going great guns until the city of Atlanta decided to ban all alcohol. The ban never went ahead, but in the lead-up to its supposed enforcement Pemberton had to find a way to keep the business going. He removed the wine from his wine coca recipe and added distilled fruit essences. The formula already had kola nut extract in it, so Pemberton called the new drink Coca-Cola. Without the wine, the thing was a real winner, not to mention a real upper. With no legislation for control of such drugs until World War I, old-fashioned and mostly ineffective tonics like vermouth were on the canvas and nearing the end of their ten-count. Then, with the twentieth century, came the rapid popularisation of the Martini, and a new role for the well-worn *wermuth*.

But who cares about vermouth when there's no gin. That's the real firepower for a good Martini: gin. And you'll need plenty of this about the place if you want to have a proper Martini party. In early Martinis gin was a much sweeter spirit, and the ratio of vermouth to gin was higher, as we've heard. A century on and the drink has evolved and dried out, if you'll pardon the pun. Indeed, the Martini of the twenty-first century is almost *beyond* dry – another reason you need the best gin you can muster.

Like vermouth, gin had been through its own near-death experience – as had a lot of the people who abused it, particularly in gin's first 150 years of life. In another similarity to vermouth, gin was also, in its beginnings, a general medicinal treatment. A Dutch professor of medicine called Franciscus de la Böe (otherwise known as Doctor Sylvius – it was sort of his stage name at the University of Leiden) invented the drink in 1650. A distillation of grains – such things as corn and barley – gin is then distilled a second time, along with its aromatic and flavouring agents – principal among which is the juniper berry. That's gin's key note. The Dutch word for juniper is *genever*, hence the diminutive form in English, *gin*. Doctor Sylvius had come up with this potion to, yes, you guessed it, treat stomach problems. The theory goes that when British soldiers on duty in Holland in the late seventeenth century saw the effects of this medicine on Dutch troops they were much impressed. Genever came to be known among the Englishmen as Dutch Courage. They must have liked the taste, too, because the English brought the drink back with them to London, where it quickly became the drink of the day – and the greatest social and economic problem of the eighteenth century. Gin. By 1729, the English Parliament had passed the first of what was to become one of many Gin Acts. Thanks to tariffs and bans on French wine, the healthy state of local corn supplies, and the high levies placed on ale, gin had become widely available and less expensive than beer. The first Gin Act aimed to place expensive licences and duties on gin in an effort to curb its terrific use. Seven years later, a new Act replaced it, banning gin altogether; but so toxic was the contraband replacement 'gin' that the Act had to be revoked. No form of control seemed to be working.

By 1750, William Hogarth had engraved *Gin Lane*. At this time the English were drinking a staggering eighty-six million litres of gin per annum – about ten times what they drink today, even though the population over those 250 years has grown tenfold. Londoners were distilling forty million litres a year. And they were drinking, on average, sixty litres of gin per capita. It is no wonder the hopelessly befuddled and ulcerated woman at the centre of Hogarth's engraving is dropping her baby, letting it fall from the stair rail into the gin bar below. She was not alone. Men were becoming impotent; women sterile; children were being born half-dead, and then either sold, murdered or left to workhouses. Those infants that survived were soon on gin themselves. Mother's Ruin: gin was the deathly opium of the people. During the 1740s in England deaths began to outnumber births. The kingdom was dying. And all because of a Dutch stomach cure . . . It was the biggest threat to life in England since the Bubonic Plague. The depressing reality of life in pre-industrial London was exacerbated by the maudlin giddiness of over-proof gin.

But then God and Parliament stepped in. Corn harvests began to suffer thanks to poor weather; and less corn meant less fuel with which to distil gin. Gin sales were affected, as were excise levies. A new Gin Act was passed, limiting the spirit's sale through such sources as distilleries, grocers, jails and workhouses. Beer was encouraged once more to be the drink of the people. More licences were granted for public and ale houses. By the 1820s gin was no longer the social and economic scourge it had been for a century. But it was a close-run thing. And that's what I mean about every Martini being a better person than you or me. The parents of the Martini, its ingredients, are two drinks that have lived a little.

Gin had to do its time, though; it wasn't until the

1880s and in slightly more reassured Victorianism that gin finally entered polite society. Whisky and cognac were drinks often served throughout dinner during this period. And that was all right for Lord Duprat-MacPhee and his cronies; but Lady Duprat-MacPhee needed something a little less powerful, or manly. Gin, being a clear, sweetish and relatively odourless spirit became the chardonnay or sauvignon blanc of the Victorian day – indeed, some hostesses referred to it as *white wine*. With the popularisation of quinine via the vector known as tonic water, gin really started to hit the heights. And then it met the Martini.

Martini di Arma di Taggia might have been mixing quite sweet original Martinis, but the taste for dryer versions didn't take long to become the norm. Prohibition and the invention of myriad cocktails (to hide the raw and poisonous flavour of so much contraband spirit) saw the Martini emerge at the end of the classic cocktail age with a very dry sense of humour indeed. Everyone's favourite drinker, Ernest Hemingway, when it came to gin versus vermouth, liked what he called the Montgomery ratio – 15:1. This ratio, by the way, was the same as the odds Monty gave for victory before going into battle.

Questions of how dry a martini should be are as divisive as the question, *Shaken or stirred?*

For dryness there are as many strange strategies and practices as there are for picking winners at the races. Pour one drop of vermouth into the otherwise empty Martini glass, swirl it around, then tip it out. Pour two drops of vermouth into the cocktail shaker, over the ice; stir it about then tip the vermouth, once again, out. Or you can adopt the advice metered out by Luis Buñuel:

Connoisseurs who like their martinis very dry suggest simply allowing a ray of sunlight to shine through a bottle of Noilly Prat before it hits the bottle of gin. At a certain period in America it was said that the making of a dry Martini should resemble the Immaculate Conception, for, as Saint Thomas Aquinas once noted, the generative power of the Holy Ghost pierced the Virgin's hymen 'like a ray of sunlight through a window – leaving it unbroken'.

Ahem.

If you are going to *actually* use some vermouth, well, there's even debate about what a drop constitutes. As one cocktail book stresses, 'the vermouth should be added as if it is the last bottle in existence'.

And then clever people – or *totally hot mixologists*, as they refer to themselves – start telling you secret secrets about substituting the vermouth to make an *even better* Martini. What tosh. Anything not made using the husband and wife team of gin and vermouth is an unMartini. A Fino Martini is one such act against God. Substitute the vermouth with fino sherry, these totally hot mixologists pretentiously proclaim. The same abuse occurs under the name Saketini – a drink that demonstrates spectacularly the awful misuse of that otherwise noble rice spirit, sake. Similarly Satanic is the Scotini, which uses Scotch whisky as the bride. Worse still is when the mixologists start trying to turn the whole world on its head by substituting *the gin*. A Rumtini is garnished with a lime twist; a Tequini is Mexico's agave plant's contribution to world peace and understanding. Of course, there is an exception that makes the rule: the Vodka Martini. But one tends to not want to disagree with 007.

Additions to the basic classic or dry Martini do not help, either. The Dirty Martini is one such problem. It's a Martini with a teaspoon or two of olive brine mixed with it. This is also sometimes known as an FDR. Yes, it was Franklin Delano Roosevelt's favourite drink. He'd shake two parts of gin, one part of vermouth, and a teaspoon of olive brine with cracked ice before straining into a glass, adding an olive just for good measure. He even fixed one of these things for Joseph Stalin in 1943, when, along with that never-too-distant Martini mascot, Winston Churchill, they met at Tehran to discuss the future of Europe and the guarantee – postwar – of Iranian sovereignty. Overlooking what must have passed through Churchill's mind at the sight of such a drink being mixed, Stalin mustn't have liked it too much. Six months later he sent Soviet troops into Azerbaijan . . .

A Gibson is another strange savoury take on the Martini. If the Dirty Martini could be likened to a desperate, dipsomaniacal Greek peasant then the Gibson is more Iberian. It's got a cocktail onion garnishing what was previously a perfectly good Dry Martini. Garnishes like onions and olives remove too much of the ethereal nothingness of the Martini; they distract from its powerful non-flavour of alcohol. Maybe a lemon twist I can come at, but even then I'm not so sure.

But what of the shaken or stirred debate?

Back to James Bond. Not only did he not want gin, but he didn't want his Vodka Martini made like a classic. Shaken, not stirred, was the disarmingly charming yet nonetheless steely reminder to any barman at any casino anywhere around the world. The nub of the problem – or the difference – is dilution. A shaken Martini is watered down, the purist will say. Here are the two methods.

Stirred. The classic treatment. Have all the ingredients almost frozen. Liquids, cocktail shaker, glass. Maybe even yourself – or whoever happens to be making the drink. (Maybe the guy that did the replicant eyes in *Blade Runner*, maybe his lab would be a good place to fix a stone-cold Dry Martini?) Over large chunks of ice in a jug, gently stir the gin and vermouth together. Strain into a Martini glass and then squeeze the oil from a twist of lemon onto the surface of the finished drink. Throw the lemon twist out, or compost it or whatever; but do not be tempted to add it to the drink. Avoid olives or their brine or cocktail onions or anything. Drink the drink immediately. This is alcohol at its transubstantiated, transcendental and transmogrified best. A stirred Martini is a Martini at its most perplexing, however. You need to drink it before it loses its icy temperature, but the wall of alcohol holds you back. Forget Sudoku, a Martini in this state will take all your powers of concentration, not to mention all your moral strength.

Or you could shake the drink.

Shaken. The convenient Martini. This is a Martini for ease and a Martini for young ladies. And most young gentlemen nowadays, come to think of it. Once again, keep everything as cold as you can – except the gin. Keep the gin at room temperature. Yes, I know this sounds ridiculous, but trust me. Over ice cubes in the shaker pour the vermouth and the gin. Shake with Amazonian vigour. Strain immediately into the frozen Martini glass. You'll now have the coldest Martini possible. The room-temperature gin has allowed the ice to break down a little, diluting the drink by maybe a tenth; but it's cold. And it's easy to drink because the temperature and the dilution have added a layer of relaxed charm to the gin, a bit like it does to us when applied in the other direction.

So if you've ever wondered why a Martini mixed for you in a swanky bar is so much nicer than the one you've laboured over to such marginally disappointing ends at home, this is the reason.

Yet even in a bar with a Martini prepared by a totally hot mixologist you can still come a cropper. Even in New York. The metaphysical Martini can be the toughest test of all.

Atalanta wasn't from Atlanta, but she sure could set a quick pace. She was one of a handful of PRs from an international hotel chain, based in New York. A New York friend, Cherry, had asked her husband, Scott, to ask Atalanta if she could guide us through a Martini tour of NYC. Another piece of information: Atalanta was also single. Cherry had spent much of the time I'd known her trying to get me to marry one of her best new friends. I don't know why that was; maybe she didn't like any of her best new friends. Or maybe she was one of those misguided if ever-so-empowered modern women who like to play mating games. It's a form of harmless twenty-first-century witchcraft. Witchcraft without the ramifications of being burnt at the stake. (That usually happens to the relationship of the couple brought together . . .)

I'd been in New York for about an hour and a half. It was January and so cold that my teeth were starting to hurt. When I got out of the cab at Cherry's building parts of my body started to shut down. The luggage on the footpath had about as much chance of independently making it up the lift to Cherry and Scott's apartment as I did. At least it was on little wheels.

I somehow lugged the gear upstairs and, through narrow hallways and lift doors, banged and bashed my way into Cherry's place. She was being typically voluble and larger than life. And she was wearing a singlet and no shoes – the apartment's heating being set to mid-August. I lost about five kilos just trying to get my jackets and gloves and shoes and socks off. We chatted and did the catch-up thing. An hour later, or about halfway through Cherry's third sentence, Scott was home. He made money go around at a big bank: whereas I used the letter buttons on a QWERTY keyboard, he used the number pad to the right. But he did have to have his hair cut quite often, and he did have to wear a tie to work.

Atalanta would meet us after dinner at something called the Flatiron Lounge – it being just a short cab ride from her apartment and a short cab ride from Cherry and Scott's. She was a fabulous girl and was crazy about Australians. That was wonderful news, but what I really wanted right now was a Martini. Scott had a similar look in his eye.

We arrived outside the Flatiron to a crowd of people queuing up. The bar's flag flew resolutely above the door, as if to say 'good luck getting in'. We jumped out of the cab and as if by some sort of strange-girl-science-fiction-ESP thinking Cherry collided with Atalanta as the latter disembarked from her yellow cab. The entire precinct threatened to implode under the power of mutual admiration and approval. 'Darling! Gorgeous! You look fabulous! I am fabulous! We are fabulous!' Scott paid the driver and then Cherry did the introduction thing. 'Atalanta, this is my friend from Australia, Ben; Ben – Atalanta. Ben writes for magazines, he's a wine writer.'

'How do you do,' I said rather lamely.

'Hello. Nice to meet you. I drink wine a lot,' she replied, more confidently.

So far so good.

But we were still on the street, and that wasn't going to do anyone any favours. However, Cherry is Jewish and she is voluble and she has curly blonde hair. Following some talking and some pointing and some smiling and some references to international journalists we went straight in. No one else with such a routine could have swung it, but that's why Cherry is Cherry, and why she is an amazing person.

We went from amazing to Art Deco. The Flatiron was in an old building constructed in 1900; the bar had been renovated to the themes of the classic cocktail era. Through the entrance archway you approach a long mahogany bar – the bar from the old ballroom. It was twenty-seven years younger than the rest of this building but it had seen the likes of the Rat Pack lean against it on more than one occasion. Low-slung lighting, blue-glass tiling, red leather booths, lots of semi-professional non-couples looking as if they'd only seen one episode of *Sex and the City*, but they'd picked up enough of the drill. We got inside and Cherry and Atalanta took off their carnival tent-like overcoats to reveal cocktail dresses composed of less material than you'd normally find in a toy parasol. We were seated and Scott said but one word: 'Martinis?'

We did four rounds in the end, and maybe it was the cocktail dresses or the jetlag or the power of a city like

New York, but each one of those Martinis saw me sitting at each point of my moral and emotional compass. North, south, east and west; I went off in every direction.

I banged the first Martini back in seconds, which was unfortunate, as I then had nothing else to do but try to stick with the conversation and ask polite open-ended questions or try to engage Scott in talk about his life or work or work or life while the girls gasbagged over virtually untouched Martinis.

But he finally caught on that something was not quite right. I'd taken another pointless sip at my very, very empty Martini glass and Scott's eye glanced for a micro-second at the alarmingly empty glass and he took a big swig at his relatively healthy glass and said: 'How about another round? Atalanta? Baby?' That was Cherry he called 'Baby', not me.

The second Martini had me more on a level playing field. The drink brought out my inner boulevardier. I talked with what I imagined to be great wit and charm about the trials and tribulations of being a true inter-national. I talked as if I were in a dinner suit, standing on the deck of a luxury cruise-ship, bringing bonhomie to all the attendant extras filling out the blank bits in the film in which I starred.

The third brought on the jetlag; but worse still, it brought out a bit of a niggling and naggling problem between Scott and Cherry. They were exchanging certain looks. They whispered a few off-stage remarks to one another when Atalanta and I seemed ensconced in thick conversation. The 'darlings' and the 'honeys' became more intoned . . .

But then Atalanta came to the rescue. She did that unbelievably wonderful thing that girls in bars sometimes do when you are drinking with them. She touched my hand. She did it without looking at me, while still in full conversational flight with Cherry, and she landed directly between my right hand's thumb and forefinger, and she squeezed my hand ever so lightly, and then she finished her sentence with Cherry and turned her head to mine and winked and then drank her Martini in one go and said, 'I think we should have more, and maybe even more after that? Like, maybe we should have a blow-out tonight?'

My left hand went straight up in the air. In it was all the money I had on me. The cocktail waitress arrived within about 1.2 seconds and I got the next round ahoy. 'Same again thanks, luv.' The waitress looked at me as if she had wasted three years studying Vietnamese. 'He means we'll have another round,' said Atalanta. 'It's his Australian accent,' added Cherry. 'Like, Ben, you're harder to understand than Cherry!' chimed in Scott. You had to be there, I guess, but we all pissed ourselves laughing.

But the fourth was my undoing. I kept getting Atalanta's name wrong. Atlanta. Juanita. I think I even called her Infanta at one stage. The Martinis were seriously derailing my evening. And everyone else's. Cherry got a look on her face. Scott was up on his feet. No, I couldn't have Atalanta's number, and no, she was going home now. Alone.

I'd not given my Martinis their deserved metaphysical respect, and I'd paid for it. And at US$100 a round, I really had.

Back in Australia, in the office, on an unseasonably cool and humidless February day, at about two minutes to lunchtime, I figured it was time to recalibrate. To get my Martini senses back into fine tune. In this sense Martini drinkers are a bit like pianos; every now and then a little man with a strange Eastern European surname and an old Gladstone bag has to be called on to get Gertie's middle C back into proper order. With Martini drinkers there's no little man to call upon, however. At least, not that I know of. You've got to set your Martini tune and time all by yourself, or perhaps with the aid of a proper bar and a proper barman. But at two minutes to lunchtime I wasn't in any position to start heading off for a consultation. So I turned to a facsimile copy of the original 1930 *Savoy Cocktail Book*, with its recipes by Harry Craddock – that magician of London's Savoy bar. Surely this man would know what to do; he was, after all, responsible for the best piece of cocktail drinking advice ever administered: 'What's the best way to drink a cocktail? Quickly, while it's still laughing at you!'

But Harry's Dry Martini recipe was very Prohibition era in style. One-third French vermouth and two-thirds dry gin. Shake it and strain it into a glass. I wasn't prepared to recalibrate by time-machine. But as I wistfully strode through the pages of the book, an old newspaper clipping fell out. A clipping I'd cut out and inserted in the book about ten years before. It was a letter, from *The Sunday Times*, written by le Comte Mosul, The Farmers Club, London, SW1. It started along the lines of 'Together with my oldest friend, Dr Robert Sainte-Ormonde, I have been mixing Gin and French for more years than I care to remember ...' It continued, 'Noilly Prat is an absolute necessity and the mixture, to allow two drinks for two imbibers, is as follows:

Into a silver cocktail shaker pour 14 measures of Plymouth Gin, add two measures of Noilly Prat, place in deep freeze the evening before use. Put wet glasses in freezer compartment of fridge and next evening pour. Add a twisted sliver of fresh lemon peel, olives are good but gentlemen use lemon, and drink fairly rapidly. The second may be consumed more slowly – depending on how imminent dinner may be. The process must be religiously performed every night for as long as necessary.

At two minutes to lunchtime on the following day, I was calibrated. And I use this recipe on the same February day every year, just to keep my body clock in tune with the Big Martini Clock in the sky.

3

Whisky, bourbon and other emergencies

I like drinking whisky and I like singing, but most people prefer to listen to me drinking whisky.
– George Burns

Scotland's Isle of Skye was more fun before they put the bridge in. You queued at the terminal at the Kyle of Lochalsh and waited for the rusty old steel and cast-iron double-open-ended car ferry to smash you through the invariably bumpy seas of the loch. It was more like a magically powered bucket than a turbine-propelled ship. Sitting in the car I kept the ignition half on, so I could use the windscreen wipers against the prevailing sea and the very light summer rain. Skye loomed on a close if ever-altering horizon. We landed at Kyleakin, near Skye's eastern tip, and did so with a ship's metal punch on a timber pier's jaw. The metaphorical hand was as sore as the metaphorical chin, however; they'd been belting each other like this for years. They were both punch-drunk. Maybe it had something to do with the whisky. But all of this was before the bridge went in. All of this was before Skye was surgically attached to the mainland of Scotland. And all of this somehow diminished what Skye's Talisker whisky meant – and now means – to me. But I'm an unrecovered romantic, and I always like things the way they used to be. Which is why I keep changing everything around so much. Trying to get the jigsaw back in its original disconfiguration. What a hopeless endeavour that is. I might as well try to dismantle the Skye Bridge.

Skye lies tucked in between the Highlands' western coast and the Western Isles. Its principal town is Portree, and I was there with a long-lost Scottish girl who wanted to see where her family had come from. Before Australians had gone to London the Scots had gone all over the world, building its railways, manning its police forces, working its farms. As stoic and as skinflint as these folk are, eventually they pop one child out who wants to see where it all started. They always fly economy, however, so the gene pool is clearly not too watered down.

We landed on Skye with a small car and two other travellers. One was a lesbian and the other one a non-lesbian who liked musicals. We'd driven from Edinburgh, each taking turns to dictate a half-hour's worth of car music and a half-hour's worth of driving. For a notoriously bad passenger, this form of torture – accompanied by the soundtracks to *Cats*, *The Phantom of the Opera* and *Les Miserables* – was fairly surreal. I think I'd formed the foetal position in the back of the little Ford by the time we'd got to the ferry. I was probably only another fifteen minutes away from understanding – in an all too practical way – why multiple murderers do what they do. No wonder I needed to make for a bar.

The long-lost Scottish girl and I checked into a B&B in Portree, just up the hill a little, but five minutes' walk from the town's old harbour and its Tolkienesque natural amphitheatre. A stern woman greeted us – if that's the right verb – at her side door and led us upstairs to a small, light, and fairly airy room, complete with a double bed and an en suite. The long-lost Scottish girl asked our hostess if there was a laundromat nearby. The hostess formed a faint, half-wry smile and told us to leave our washing; she would happily do it later that night. A deposit was exchanged for a key and a few minutes later I saw our hostess driving away in a small car and a nurse's uniform. At least the washing would be properly and thoroughly cleaned.

The long-lost Scottish girl wanted to have a rest; a lie down. I wanted to get to the bar and obliterate the recurring nightmare that was the car trip and the musical non-music. She went all silent on me, so I figured it best to heave off before things got any worse.

Finding a pub in a new town – whether you are a tourist or a business traveller or whatnot – is always pretty easy. There are two methods. Ask the first person you see with a twinkle in their eye. Or, if you don't speak the language, go on intuition. The better you are at drinking, the better your intuition will be. This is why half-arsed, try-hard occasional drinkers can never find a pub or a bar when they need to, even on a Friday night in Vegas.

But back to Scotland and Portree. I wandered without a care or a drink down the narrow streets towards the harbour, my pace gathering. From the rise above and opposite the water you could make out three or four pubs where fishermen once restored their vigour after tackling (or, perhaps, even before venturing into) the Sound of Raasay. Making my way around to the harbour from my vantage point I walked past an old pub; an old man was pushing his way into it, via an old door. I followed. The dark bar was darkly lit and the only inhabitants were three other old men plus the new old man and the barman – and little old me. There was barely the sound of a working, trading pub to be heard. The old bloke ordered a half-pint of Gillespies Stout and a Talisker whisky chaser. He settled in with the other old men and I repeated his order to the barman, who batted not one eyelid. The drill was a simple one. You sat there with your half-pint for as long as you could. Possibly for as long as it took for the stout to evaporate. Once the stout had either been drunk or it had indeed evaporated you dealt with the whisky in three or four deft blows, drinking it with a natural yet suppressed glee, like a broadsword cutting through English chain mail.

Knowing I didn't have the whisky-built immortality of the old blokes, I fast-tracked the rest of the experience and started to drink the stout and the whisky at a fairly similar and high speed – and perhaps even concurrently. I had driven from Edinburgh, however, and I had listened to some of the finest moments from contemporary music-hall soundtracks on the way. None of these old blokes would have had a morning like that. The old boys weren't in this pub to put flight to fear or care. It was just what they did. The stout was like porridge to them; the whisky was like mother's milk. Indeed, as Mark Twain once commented, 'Scotch whisky to a Scotsman is as innocent as milk is to the rest of the human race.' A few drinks later I figured – what with me not being Scots – it was time to take in Portree's other highlights. But as I left the pub the RAF attacked. Two jets flew over the town about an inch and a half above the top of my head and about an inch and a half apart. Both seemed at full throttle, and as I ran down the street looking for cover they shot straight back over the town. Then I heard a strange and indecipherable voice proclaiming something of intense importance; and then I turned the corner and fell into the plush, deep-green, grassy amphitheatre that was the geographic magic of Portree.

It was the Highland Games.

The amphitheatre was mostly surrounded by locals and visitors and the caravan that is Highland Gaming's regular personnel. Body-builders and very tall fat blokes – all in kilts – strode about tossing cabers, throwing hammers, and putting shots. And wearing ridiculous beards. One team looked a little odd, however, probably because the last of their lot was my girlfriend. She was on the end of a line of very handsome ladies pulling for tug-of-war victory. The Isle of Skye Ladies' Lifeboat Team was one short, and my long-lost Scottish girl was somehow in the wrong place at the wrong time. It was the final and the Ladies' Lifeboat Team mechanically pulled their helpless opposition across the line, with the long-lost Scottish girl acting as little more than a passenger on a huge rope. She could hardly get her hands around it.

The Ladies' Lifeboat Team accepted the perpetual trophy. They'd won it now for the last three years. And each member of the team received a half-bottle of Famous Grouse. As the long-lost Scottish girlfriend accepted her prize, she turned to the crowd and her eyes suddenly fixed on me. She held the half-bottle aloft and shook it from side to side, as if to say, 'This is mine!' She ran across the lush, green field of the amphitheatre as the men's tug-of-war teams prepared. 'Look what I've won! Look what I've won!' she shouted. Feeling finally and fully Scottish she took the top off the bottle and had a swig. For a girl who barely drank she did so like a seasoned professional. We sat on the banks of the amphitheatre and watched the men tug away, so to speak. The final was an epic and when some visiting Canadians won, the crowd of visitors erupted. The winning Canadians received their prizes – *full* bottles of Famous Grouse. The long-lost Scottish girl bristled. 'That's not fair!' she whined. Equality of the sexes had clearly not made it to Portree. But, then again, they did have a Ladies' Lifeboat Team. It's certainly the only one I've ever met.

That night we met up in town with the lesbian and the non-lesbian for dinner. We ate some of the worst food I've ever had; but everyone in the pub loved it because it was the Highland Games and we were on Skye and a peculiar sense of happiness had descended. When our sausages and potato thing arrived it was delivered by a woman with billowing arms. She plonked the meals down on doily-seated under-plates and looked at the long-lost Scottish girl: 'Aren't you the wee lassie from this afternooooooooon?' So we had a Highland Games reunion meeting after the dinner and we drank and drank and drank Talisker and the next morning I thought the most sensible thing to do was to take the car and go over to the distillery – to see from where my new dietary staple came from.

Talisker lies near Cnoc nan Speireag, or Hawkhill, close to the village of Carbost, on the shore of Loch Harport. Loch Harport runs to Loch Snizort, which leads out into the Sea of the Hebrides. Anyone who has ever read a Dr Seuss book will fall instantly in love with the place names. And possibly the whisky.

Talisker has died many deaths. It has, however, always managed to come back to life, and in this sense it is like one of those old men in Portree – the whisky immortals. The men who could drink it all day long; sometimes falling and failing but always coming back – ever so loyally – for more.

Sitting on the shore of Loch Harport, Talisker, as an architectural feature, looks like something crossed between a port-maker's quinta and a crofter's cottage – and built by both men after they'd been on the grog for a few days. Long, barn-like buildings; small, dark windows, and a single word – TALISKER – marked along the whitish wall facing the loch. It was built in 1830 by two brothers – Hugh and Kenneth MacAskill – and over the following 150 years it merged, expanded, burnt down, and bits of it have even been demolished. Talisker was Robert Louis Stevenson's favourite single malt; and Boswell and Dr Johnson got on the whisky here, at nearby Talisker House. According to Boswell's record, Johnson thought Talisker whisky better than English brandy. And the doctor, by bulk of experience, probably knew it to be so. Talisker itself is a word that comes from the Old Norse. Vikings crashed regularly into the inner and outer Hebrides, and the stone and rubble cairns that dot the tiny promontories of the Isle of Skye remind anyone who cares to let their mind so wander about that old Nordic threat. Indeed, eerie, long and thin runnels in the soft rock of some of the island's loch shores hint at the powerful and deadly arrival of longships – their metal-covered keel board cutting into the island as they landed.

Thalas Gair is Norse for Sloping Rock, a mountain near to Talisker House – the seat of the island's clan Macleod. Which probably explains why most of the people at Talisker's distillery have the surname Macleod.

Talisker isn't made so differently to any other whisky, because all whisky – even when it's whiskey or bourbon – start out life as a rough beer. Water, grain and yeast are the ingredients, and each one lends a layer of complexity and personality to the finished spirit. The grain is malted, then it's mashed; fermentation takes place before the process of distillation furthers the equation, with the distiller playing a key role in accentuating high and low notes, not to mention strength. Cask ageing and – in about 90 per cent of all whiskies – blending finish off the job. In this sense whisky has many similarities to wine, for while both can be made under revolting industrial applications, both can also – when at their best – be strange liquid connections to their place of origin: its environment, its produce, and to the people who make the stuff. Indeed, some whisky-makers reckon that the water they use is equivalent to a winemaker's grapes – it's the starting point for definition, character and style in a whisky.

Which leads us to another similarity – but this time back to beer. Before massive technological and industrial change took place, breweries were always to be found bang-smack next to a good freshwater source. Whether Czechoslovakian, English or Tasmanian, all of the old and traditional breweries were literally on top of springs or baths, rivers or lakes. Water quality and, more importantly, water minerality, taints and softness put a real thumbprint on the finished beverage. If we skip back to wine once more, we see this very clearly, too: pumped water irrigation on some vineyards in South Australia has affected natural water tables and led to higher levels of salinity in the soil. And in the grapes that grow there . . .

Talisker's water is decidedly peaty. It flows through peat at Cnoc nan Speireag, but its pungency isn't something the people of Skye note with too much concern. Spring water on the island can often look like a weak cup of tea. The water too has something of the sea in it. There's an essence of marine life, as there is in the whisky; but there's a touch of that quality in almost everything on Skye, particularly on this wet and exposed side of the island. Standing on the seaweed on the shore of Lake Harport, with the prevailing wind and sea bringing in the naturopathic smells and tastes from the Gulf Stream, you get an overwhelming sense that nature is having its way with this whisky – and with you.

Besides the water that goes to make whisky needing to be relatively neutral, it also needs to be cold. Not only is water used in malting and mashing, but it is also used to cool the still's condensers at the distillation stage – but we are a beer-brew away from that yet.

Grain. Depending on which country you're in, different grains play different and sometimes very vital roles in the final body and taste of whisky. While single malt is made only from barley, whiskies in general (and we include such things as Irish and American whisky) can form from a range of grains and cereals: corn is probably the most common, and rye and wheat are used in lower proportions, excepting in the US, where they still play a strong role in bourbon, Tennessee and rye whisky. The Irish even use small amounts of oats in their pure pot still releases. That certainly gives a new angle to breakfast.

In single malt whisky, the barley first has to be malted. It is soaked in water for a few days, during which it is turned over to help lift the humidity. Once the grain has reached a soaked stage ready for germination, it is spread out over malting floors at a thickness of up to a half-metre. Here it is once again turned over and over, using wooden shiels, which are otherwise known as whisky shovels. As the temperature of the germinating barley rises, the layer is spread out further and further, lowering its height. Germination, of course, turns starch into sugar. And the semi-spongy, floury barley is now called green malt. Off it then goes to the kiln for drying, and to stop any further germination. It is spread out over a perforated floor, which allows the smokiness of the smouldering peat underneath to permeate the grain. Peat fuel for kilning green malt is only part of the entire fuel regime. Indeed, most whisky is now made using mechanised and automated systems, whereby malting and germination can both occur inside one vat. The particular quality that peat smoke brings to single malts ranges from medicinally herbal to peculiarly marine. The islands of the west coast of Scotland have peat that is highly compacted and contains as much decayed sea-weed and salt as it does heather and moss. Talisker has an integrated peatiness; but for a mind-blowing and medicinal peat explosion you need to head to Islay and its famous (and unforgettable) Laphroaig.

Once the grain has malted down to about 5 per cent water content, it is ground and mashed with hot water. The idea is to release the fermentable starch. In tanks, the ground malt is washed with three doses of water – some of which is saved over from the last mash. A little bit like sour mash whisky, or sourdough bread . . .

The effect of the washing is to create a wort. Yes, another beer term. Fermented in wooden or stainless-steel containers called washbacks, the yeast is now added to the wort. And it is then paddled, or constantly muddled, in an effort to keep fermentation temperatures low. Distiller's yeast is a fairly hardy thing, but if it gets above about 35°C it can tire, and even die. So the fermentation period is fairly long – maybe five days. And at the end of this time, yes, you have a malty beer of around 7 per cent alcohol by volume. Apparently it can be drunk; but it's a bit of an acquired taste . . .

Which is why it is better to distil it. Twice.

Single malt begins its journey from odd beer to sublime spirit in a pot still. These are big copper vessels that often look a bit Arabic, which isn't so odd because that's where distilling started – centuries before Catholic monks brought distilling to Scotland and Ireland, the Arabs were using the technique to make perfumes and tonics, as opposed to the water of life. These big pots funnel upwards through their swan necks to condensing pipes. Operating a still is a bit like boiling a kettle. The liquid inside is heated up and it evaporates (and pretty smartly, too, as alcohol boils at a lower temperature than water); the rising gas funnels out into the condensing pipes and changes from gas back to liquid. The lighter vapours make the journey out easily; but the heavy gases drop back into the still where they have to go through the evaporative process all over again. After the alcoholic contents of the kettle have been boiled off, the rough beer has, via evaporation and condensation, been turned into low wine. That's the silly term the distiller uses for this strange brew – and a brew at about 25 per cent alcohol by volume at this stage (some low wine . . .). This low wine now goes into a smaller still for the second distillation, and this is where the distiller makes his money. He pulls shots. The foreshots flow out of this final distillation first. They're high in alcohol and high in aromatics and aldehydes. And highly undrinkable. Like pastis, they also turn cloudy when mixed with water. The more fore-shots the stillman runs from the still the stronger the middle cut will be – the part of the second distillation that will form the final drink. Run off more foreshots and you get a cleaner, lighter whisky. But the job's not over with that. The end of the distillation sees final shots called feints appear. These are more smoky and sul-phurous. It's the fine lines that the distiller runs at both sides of the middle cut that determine the flavour, weight, and structure of the final whisky; but there's some cosmetic treatment and relaxation therapy to go through first. Young whisky straight from the still is colourless and a little uptight. And about 70 per cent alcohol by volume. Which is why it is diluted a touch before it goes into barrels.

Oak casks are enshrined in whisky law. You've got to put your colourless baby whisky into an oak cask for a period of ageing – a minimum of three years. All sorts of oak is used, some old and some new. Traditionally, second-hand sherry casks were used. They can be up to 500 litres in capacity and are made out of anything from European oak to chestnut wood. And their CV might include work with such robust sherries as oloroso or amontillado. Imagine a young Scots boy being educated in a Spanish school for three years and you'll understand the effect these casks can have on the whisky. Indeed, it's from cask ageing that whisky picks up its colour and roundness, plus a lot of its richer flavours. These rich and almost sweet characters are accentuated even more loudly when American oak casks are used for whisky maturation. Left over from bourbon ageing, these barrels are smaller in size (maybe 200 litres) and their oak is more porous. Its flavour characters are also sweeter than European oak, so they impart vanilla notes to the whisky encased by them. Of course, being smaller barrels, there's a greater wood-to-whisky ratio. And many of them have also been lightly toasted over oak fires, to lend some empyreumatic qualities to the whisky, just for good measure.

But the cask doesn't own the agenda all by itself. Where the warehouse lies is another important factor. Colder whisky regions in the Highlands or on the islands make for greater humidity in the storage warehouses. This means that some alcohol evaporates from the porous barrels, drifting off towards Heaven. No wonder this alcohol loss is called *the angels' share*. In warmer regions with dryer warehouses what is lost over time is not alcohol but water. It evaporates, lowering the casks' volume. In contrast, the casks in colder regions, while losing a little bit of alcohol, don't tend to drop in volume ... The whisky in the casks will also pick up any local atmospheric and aromatic peculiarities – such as Talisker's seaweediness.

Out of the barrel, the whisky is once more cut back with water, to even out the alcohol strength, back to the low 40 per cents. Filtered and bottled, the responsibility for this drink now lies with you. And it's no easy task.

Single malt needs only one thing once you get it in the glass: a drop or two of water. On Skye, there was plenty of native stuff on tap, so to speak, and Talisker's enjoyment was therefore easy and natural. And strangely forgiving, too. When I drink whisky in such quantities anywhere but Scotland, things happen that shouldn't happen. At least not to me. So I went to a lot of trouble to try and link something natural and easy within me with such a drink as single malt Scotch whisky. I was convinced there was something magical – and therefore redeeming – about a perfect glass of single malt whisky and a perfect drop or two of spring water – in all its simple and pure glory, as Mother Nature had intended.

I returned home to Australia, to the place where I grew up. To the forest across the road. Twenty thousand hectares of cold, high-altitude rainforest. To a mossy rock wall above a tiny, fern-lined creek; from the rock jutted a spring, which trickled into the running water below. A kid at primary school had once told me that the spring water took 2000 years to get from the top of the mountain to the mossy rock wall halfway down. This kid's dad was a forest ranger, so, naturally enough, we all believed him. And although I was on the opposite side of the world from the Isle of Skye, I was sure this 2000-year-old spring water would speak truths to the Talisker whisky. One antipodean to another; deep speaking to deep. I collected the spring water in a stainless-steel hiking canister. The water was very soft, and very neutral. My confidence was high. All I had to do now was pour the whisky correctly. Yes, it is not just a simple matter of pulling the stopper out and banging the spirit in any old glass. A good glass of single malt and its preparation is surrounded by nearly as much brouhaha as a Japanese tea ceremony – I know, because I've tried such a ceremony. Besides, without ceremony and correct whisky form, you might as well buy a bottle of cheap bourbon and go kangaroo shooting.

I'd used this two-millennium water before. Once when trying to make the perfect cup of tea, and once while trying to make the perfect home-brewed beer. That my house was on tank water from rainfall probably made this a bit irrelevant, but making tea – and beer – from spring water, tank water, and – the final part of the comparative experiment – chlorinated, fluoridated water seemed like something worthwhile to do; particularly when you had a lonely Easter at home, your knee in a brace (my first and last football injury), and all your friends away for holidays. Hobbling through the scrub on one and a half legs in order to get the two-thousand-year-old water was but the start of the fun.

The water made absolutely no perceptible difference to any of the home-brewed beers. They were three pale ales that all tasted uniformly dull and lumpy. Ninety-odd bottles of beer marked either TAP, TANK or SPRING were that winter drunk off, usually at parties, usually at about midnight, usually after the commercial beer had run out. And the cask wine. And the marijuana. And the music videos. It was desperate beer for a desperate situation. It would've been the last thing they turned to in the Black Hole of Calcutta. I mean the Dimly Lit Cellar of Madras.

But to the tea I was sure this water would make all the difference. Following what I imagined to be a painstakingly accurate Japanese tea ceremony procedure, I felt that the water would help me get it right, to seize, as the Japanese put it, the *ichi-go ichi-e* – the one chance in my lifetime to bring my universe into complete harmony.

The minutiae of *Cha-no-yu*, or hot water for tea, can make assembling a sugar cube by dipsomaniacal hand while wearing a blindfold look straightforward. The emphasis in a tea ceremony is all about service, however, which is why I figured I needed to get someone to watch and to be, eventually, served the tea. With no one around and no one at home my guest was therefore the five-year-old depressed German Shepherd, Ernie. He'd been the runt of a litter of impressive, prize-winning dogs, but had somehow missed out on mental acuity. He was handsome enough, but given to a few psychological problems. No wonder my mother agreed to take him from the distraught breeder. He sort of fitted in with the rest of our family, and all too well.

So Ernie sat and watched as I went through the ritual of making him *Cha-no-yu*, albeit in a dog bowl, not a teacup. I used as a guide the etiquette of Murata Shuko, the father of Japanese Teaism. It's all very Zen. Meditative, natural and spiritual graces flow both through and from traditional social values based around hospitality and politeness. My aim, according to the Teaists, was to serve tea in such a way that there was nothing to notice. Ernie seemed quite interested, however. To bring authenticity and precision to the ceremony I wore one of those cotton Japanese-print non-kimono sort of dressing gowns. And a pair of rubber thongs, which was the closest footwear I had to the more traditional Japanese tea-service clog. I also bought some Japanese tea, called 'Japanese Green Tea', from the supermarket. I went to the supermarket well before the tea ceremony, and dressed in jeans and a shirt, not in the kimono. Not that I hadn't been to supermarkets in dressing gowns before, but the last time I'd done that was on the way to the drive-in, and I was six.

A tea ceremony can hinge on any one of myriad factors, none of which seem to have much to do with the tea. Geography, architecture and furnishings can make or break it. So I chose the back room of the house, which was north-facing. Lots of natural light, no bathroom or toilet, a pretty view of the garden, and a fish pond. The garden even had a few dozen Japanese maples in it. Like, how Japanese could it get?

The positioning and the preparation of the tea equipment was the next problem. Once again I reckoned I had this covered, as, being a fairly anal person, I like things just so. In the right place. Being Aries means that I know how the teacup (or dog bowl) and the kettle and the tea-leaf pot and the weird little bamboo tea-leaf whisk I'd bought from one of those posh homewares stores should sit on the low coffee table I'd brought into the room to serve the tea on. For the German Shepherd.

The coffee table irked my Zen harmony. But as my second-favourite TV character of all time (Tripitaka, from the oddly coincidental Japanese TV show of the 1980s, *Monkey*) would have said, *Is not a coffee table just a table that is low to the ground? Cannot a table have as many guises as Buddha, and can Buddha ever be wrong?*

But now I was mixing my Zen with my Buddhism when I should have been mixing the tea and concentrating on not letting the dog notice that I was making the tea, not that he seemed a problem at the minute, at least to the perfect nature of my tea ceremony. He was now lying on the floor, with his two front paws crossed one over the other, his jaw resting on them, his eyes long and muted, as if his doggy mind were trying to suppress something sad about his mother or his siblings – or maybe he was just being a bit German and didn't much like this poor-taste joke of my Japanese tea ceremony. (Come to think of it, he did seem much more interested in the beer brewing . . .)

I wasn't sure if music was appropriate or not, and the closest two recordings we had to anything remotely Japanese was Bizet's 'The Pearl Fishers' and James Galway's greatest flute hits – bits of which reminded me of the incidental music in another TV show, *Kung Fu*. So I passed on the music, although Ernie did like 'The Pearl Fishers' quite a lot, particularly when Zurga the temple priest let rip in powerful baritone, telling the bleating tenor – appropriately enough named Nadir – to stay away from his former and secret girlfriend, Leila. Yes, all very *Home and Away*. It's even set on a beach, albeit a Ceylonese one.

Once you get to the stage where the water has boiled, Zen tea-making moves into a higher gear. The amount of tea and the tea's nature; the type and temperature of the water; the speed and time of the whisking: all of these things determine whether you've made thin tea (called *usucha*) or thick tea (*koicha*). Thin tea and thick tea require slightly different drinking procedures, of course. I couldn't work out if my tea was thick or thin. It certainly wasn't milky, or strained, or sugared, which, according to most people in the postcode, meant it wasn't tea at all. Gently resting the whisk back down on the table I presented the dog bowl of *usucha/koicha* to Ernie, remembering I had to do this in such a way that he wouldn't notice. So graceful and polite would my virtually invisible presentation of the tea be to him that he would, in failing to notice me serve it to him, thank me in tones of supreme understatement and noble inscrutability. The way Ernie handled (or pawed) the dog-tea-bowl; the way he sipped (or gulped) the tea; and the way he appreciated it and the equipment used to prepare it and the nature of my invisible service would be the final line in the complex yet perfect equation that was a Japanese tea ceremony. Bowing and placing the bowl before his crossed paws and long face, I retreated three backward steps to the coffee table – I mean the tea table – and politely awaited his appreciation of the tea. We waited. He raised himself up on two good and two prematurely arthritic legs and had a sniff at the bowl. He took one half-swipe at the tea's surface with his tongue, glancing up at me as he did so. He licked the sides of his mouth a couple of times, sort of smiled at me and made one of those playful barks, throwing his nose up into the air. He then went straight outside and had a wee. I hate to think what he would have done if I'd not gone to all the bother of getting that 2000-year-old spring water.

Figuring the ancient water had done the trick with my one and only Japanese tea ceremony, I was sure it would bring something ethereal to bear on my Talisker single malt Scotch whisky. But maybe some form of ceremony and thought was required before I opened the bottle and got on it. If time, place, procedure and utensils could make or break a tea ceremony, what could they do to a glass of single malt?

The glass was one place to start. Tradition dictates that a short glass with angled sides is what you pour your whisky into. It's a lumpy little glass with a thick base. They are often quite heavy glasses, too. Perhaps that's their single point of merit: after you've drunk a half-bottle of whisky and you drop the glass, it doesn't smash; it doesn't even chip; and it doesn't roll away too far. Meritorious or not, that's not really the point, though. Pompous connoisseurship of single malts does not lead to any form of drunkenness in any way whatsoever. That's impossible. This is why it's better to find a glass for your whisky that's going to accentuate the deeper and more complex aromatic qualities of the spirit. Even if the glass is an $85 mouth-blown, hand-made Austrian lead-crystal one, such as those ones built by the posh *par excellence* stemware manufacturer, Riedel. These Riedel whisky glasses are delicate creatures. They tend to mysteriously break whenever you try to corral them towards the sink; they develop cracks whenever you take a clean, linen, glass-drying towel out of the cupboard. And their rims tend to shape out, not in. They are the shape of a flower in late bloom; they are not tulip-shaped, a shape which helps to funnel aroma. In fact, the Riedel whisky glass seemed like a bit of a compromise vessel. Its shape funnelled about two-thirds of the way up the glass before blossoming outwards right at the rim-edge. The basic theory when it comes to an ideal whisky glass is that it will have a big-enough bowl to let the whisky undergo some subtle aeration, but have a narrow-enough opening so as to underplay the toxic shock of 40+ per cent alcohol. You want a glass that funnels the finer aromatics; which is probably why I use a small, tulip-shaped wine glass. Wine glasses are amazingly useful delivery devices for so many things: beer (in the form of good ale), whisky, brandy, Calvados, Armagnac, and – sometimes – even wine.

With glass specifications meeting our exacting standards we now find ourselves at the point of service and subsequent receipt of said whisky. Yes, I agree with you; by now most sane people would have given up. Time and place when it comes to whisky are to me fairly straightforward concepts: at home and at night. After dinner. Or sometimes during dinner, if dinner isn't going too well. Not from your point of view, of course; but from the point of view of anyone unlucky enough to be dining with you in one of your cranky moods. Some things are obvious, however: drinking whisky after dinner makes for restful sleep. Just as long as you go to bed and do not go out. Drinking whisky before dinner is pretty much for regimented officers on leave who also happen to be secondary characters in a Jane Austen novel. Anyone who is alive today and, as a real person, actually drinks whisky before dinner needs to understand this, and they need to understand they are living anomalies. (Congratulations, by the way.) Drinking whisky at afternoon tea is a worrying sign; that's all I will say about that. Drinking whisky after lunch means you will need to get used to a very different sleep regime. And drinking whisky either before lunch or at breakfast – or before breakfast – is only for people at war. Or home from war. I am not going to sit here and tell a returned serviceman, or woman, what is proper when it comes to drink.

But I will tell them one thing. Water. A drop or two of water. But never tap water. That defeats the purpose. You can go to extremes, of course, as I guess I had done by trekking through the bush to get to the spring in order to fill a stainless-steel one-litre hiking canister with its trickle. Some people take it further. They ship water from the source. Scottish spring water. It goes all over the world – to the US, to Japan, to Italy – to allow the single-malt addicts within those whisky-loving countries to savour their drug of choice as they see fit. There's an argument for and against, of course.

It starts with the notion of cask-strength whisky. This is spirit at just above 60 per cent alcohol. At bottling it is cut back with distilled local water to about 40 per cent, which is where most whisky – whether single malt or some supermarkets' '1000 Sporrans Special' home-brand – sits. When bottled, the whisky is also chill-filtered, to remove any cask deposits or fattier by-products of ageing. Malt-whisky fans reckon this only removes flavour, and does nothing to improve the final drink. More arguing ensues. Just as it does with the drop or two of water.

If a distiller has settled on his final blend of single malt and decreed it is a perfect balance of flavour to texture, then why add a drop of water when you've got it back in your lounge room on the other side of the world? To help release aroma and to help ease flavour, that's why. A drop or two of water sets off some of the bottled whisky's volatiles, and takes the edge off the alcohol's sting. The drink subsequently smells more and tastes better. So why wouldn't you drop a drop or two in the glass? If for no other reason than for the procedural element; and the romance; and for the same reasons that I, all those years ago, carried out a Japanese tea ceremony for a depressed German Shepherd.

I drank my Talisker from a sherry copita. Sipping it; savouring it. I drank a second copita's worth, but this time with two drops of my two-thousand-year-old spring water added. There was absolutely no perceivable difference. Yet I would never drink single malt again without the addition of those two drops of water. If such water, even in a tea ceremony, could make a depressed pure-breed dog happy, well, that was all the evidence I needed. Style over substance *can* have meaning. Unless you find yourself at a Jack Daniels' sales pitch – I mean, tasting. But bourbon isn't whisky; it's alcoholic cornmeal.

Oscar Mendelsohn's dictionary of drink and drinking (published in 1965, and, in most cases, a reassuringly old-fashioned sort of reference book) cites bourbon thus:

> Bourbon Whiskey: American spirit (known as corn whiskey) legally required to be made from not less than 51% maize and aged in charred white-oak barrels. The name is derived from Bourbon County in Kentucky, where corn whiskey was supposed to have been first made. Choice, matured bourbon whiskey has a superb bouquet and is one of the great spirits of the world.

Poppycock. It's corn alcohol and you can always taste corn alcohol when you drink it; and on the odd occasion you *can't* taste the corn alcohol you can taste American oak barrel flavours, which, to any sensible grown-up person, always tastes like rum 'n' raisin ice-cream, vanilla, and confectionery. No wonder children like this stuff. Or maybe that's just the American taste? The sweetness didn't seem to be a problem to Brown-Forman's master distiller, Chris Morris, a Kentucky native and internationally renowned bourbon expert. He thought the sweetness was to be admired. Indeed, in the *vocabulary of bourbon*, as he put it, rich and sweet smells and flavours dominate.

The first area is 'Sweet Aromatics'. These come from the 100 per cent toasted barrels; we get honeycomb and candy aromas. The second area is 'Spice': here we have brown spice like nutmeg and green spice like spearmint and anise. The third area of flavour is 'Fruit and Floral' – everything from apple to figs. The fourth area is 'Wood'. Charred oak and nuts and, well, wood flavours . . . The final area of flavour, the fifth area, is 'Grain'.

Corn, rye, malt. Candy, spearmint, apples, malt. All sweet and all harmonised by the effects of charred oak; like a fire that has gone through a children's playground and singed all the treated-pine play equipment. The burnt lignin in the timber caramelise. When the end product of this alchemy is bourbon, well, no wonder testosterone-filled young adults love the stuff. It's like a liquid confectionery bar, with the liquid taking the form of 40 per cent alcohol, and the smells reminding them of the playgrounds not so far removed from powerful emotional memory.

'The barrels we build at our Bluegrass Cooperage come from the trees we grow,' says Morris. *Quercus alba*, or white oak. The timber matures for nine months outside, then one-inch-thick barrels are made. The oak tannins in the wood break down into a red colour; and the lignin break down into vanilla flavour. Add to this the fact that the inside of the barrels are charred at over 1500° Fahrenheit (850°C). A sixteenth of an inch of that timber is burnt away, and the charred cellulose breaks down into ten different types of sugar. Hence all bourbon's chocolate, butterscotch, candy and so on flavours . . .

73

I was starting to feel a little bit sugary-Shakespearean, whereby a little and a little is too much. The thought of these sweet flavours, and the master distiller's wondrous passion for them, and for the miracle that was their making, had me on a post-sugar-high downward curve. And we still had to taste the bourbon.

It was Woodford Reserve. Before we got to drink it, though, we had to see it in its freshly distilled guise, before it went into those brand-new charred-oak barrels. It was a clear spirit (just as freshly distilled single malt is) and in Kentucky it goes by the name White Dog. And it smelt like particularly fruity grappa. All spice and fruit. What a shame they had to turn it into confectionary.

Morris explained the Woodford Reserve process. It starts, like whisky, with the water. 'Woodford is made from water from Glenn's Creek, which feeds into the Kentucky River. It is water high in calcium, which is good for horse bones, which is why so many good horses come from Kentucky. And why so much good whisky does too.'

Woodford is also a sour mash – like bourbon is, and like Tennessee whisky is. But it uses a lower proportion of leftover mash from the last fermentation. Woodford is about 6 per cent used, or sour, mash. (Once again, very similar to some single malts.)

'One strain of yeast is used, which makes a huge, congener-laden spirit, full of flavour. That's what we want, lots of congeners.' In order to get them, Woodford is fermented over seven days (four days longer than most bourbons) in cypress wood fermenters. A beer of 9 per cent alcohol is produced, which is subsequently triple-distilled before going into the barrel. 'The wood soaks up about three gallons of whisky,' reckoned

Morris, quite proudly. 'It's like dunking a teabag in water, the barrel being the teabag . . .'

Morris was kind enough to smell the Woodford and then take a sip before telling the assembled tasters what it was they would taste. 'Smooth, mild, not a bit of alcohol on the nose; toffee, tobacco leaf, black pepper to the taste; the finish is smooth and cherried.'

I tried the spirit. It was all alcohol heat and burn. The black pepper effect was there, but it was also burning and unpleasant.

'Woodford Reserve has 51 per cent of the small-batch bourbon market share,' added Morris, 'and the reason for that – as you can see for yourselves – is its amazing complexity. It's the most complex bourbon, in fact, with 212 flavour compounds . . .'

Clearly my tasting glass was missing 211 of them. Or maybe I was missing something. I asked an old cowboy-type at the tasting what was wrong with me and bourbon, why we couldn't understand each other, let alone like one another's company.

'You've got to go to bed with your boots on,' was his reply. I wanted to see how that was an answer, but I must admit struggling a little bit with the searingly obvious logic of it all. I looked at him searchingly.

'Drinking bourbon requires one man and one bottle of bourbon. And one pair of cowboy boots. Snakeskin, rawhide – that doesn't matter so much. Once you've drunk the bottle of bourbon you'll probably need to go to bed, Kentucky style, with your boots on. Only a fool would try to take their boots off after drinking a bottle of bourbon.'

I'd be surprised if I could even find the bed. But excess via a bottle of bourbon per man per night shouldn't seem so surprising to anyone who's been to Kentucky. Bourbon County is but one of 120 counties in the state. And it is a county that's home to, nowadays, *no* distilleries. It's also a dry county. You can't get a drink of whisky in Bourbon County. You can't get a drink of *bourbon* in Bourbon County. No wonder you have to drive to another county, buy a bottle of bourbon, check into a motel room, and drink it until your boots won't come off. If you can't drink it at the source, why drink it anywhere else around the world? Do all the Bourbon County locals go home to prayer group and laugh their heads off at what they've done? And why sell it to the world with so much vigour when you can't drink it at home? Bourbon distillers need a big mirror . . .

4

Instant lift-off: the cocktail hour

The trouble with the world is that everybody in it
is three drinks behind.
– Humphrey Bogart

Cool, clear, clean and careful connoisseurship of high-class beverages such as champagne and fine wine might be the mark of the cultural elite, but such drinks so politely consumed lack acceleration. Sometimes you need to get through the ionosphere and out into deep space – or at least into orbit – fairly quickly. You need instant lift-off. Dorothy Parker might be quite right about the cocktail party: 'I misremember who first was cruel enough to nurture the cocktail party into life. But perhaps it would be not too much to say, in fact it would be not enough to say, that it was not worth the trouble.' But the cocktail *hour* is an entirely different and much more enjoyable labour. Even if you're labouring it all by yourself.

The best thing about the cocktail hour is its ability to

put burden and worry to flight. A Martini, a Pink Gin, a Perfect Manhattan; a Kir Royale, a Margarita, a Pimm's Cup. Make but one of these drinks and serve it to all and sundry and suddenly the night (or afternoon) looks after itself. In fact, I will go further than that: part of the reason Class-A drug use has become so popular with young people of late is because they were never allowed to drink proper cocktails. All sixteenth birthday parties should be cocktail parties. At least it might encourage better dress sense, not to mention conversation.

It's not as simple as that, of course it's not. That's because there are *right* cocktails and there are *wrong* cocktails. And this is even before we have worked out how to say the word in the first place. *Cocktail* is pronounced *co-tail*. This pronunciation has no pretentiousness attached to it at all; it's simply the way the word is correctly enunciated. Ask anyone partaking of a co-tail at a co-tail party – whether they are young ladies in co-tail dresses or captains of business in dinner suits, I mean *dinner suets* – ask any one of them if they'd like a *cocktail* as opposed to a *co-tail* and you will quickly come to a very complete understanding of how important it is to get the pronunciation right. Right pronunciation; right co-tails; right people. This is what it is all about.

Seriously, any further stubborn concerns you have about enjoying a co-tail as opposed to a cocktail should be banished immediately. The word itself has no firm etymological birthday or place, at least as far as its meaning where drinks are concerned goes. Its first recorded usage is in New York in 1806: *A cocktail, then, is a stimulating liquor, composed of spirits of any kind, sugar, water, and bitters.* One of the noun's other meanings is more interesting: *A person assuming the position of a gentleman, but deficient in thorough gentlemanly breeding.* Such a cocktail would no doubt drink cocktails, not co-tails. It's one way to pick them . . .

Wrong co-tails. They certainly exist. Or, as we might more suitably term them, wrong COCKtails. Yes, far too many of these conCOCKtions ruin the evenings of far too many young people. And it is because these cocktails are not appetisers. Co-tails get things moving in the general direction of stylish enjoyment; COCKtails take over the entire night, from anxious early arrivals to 9.30 pm toilet-cubicle sex and vomiting. Their consumption is akin to eating a badly made commercial pavlova before dinner, under the appalling misapprehension that this is what the locals do. It is *when-in-Rome* logic applied in the most unfortunate way. And all because no one has ever bothered to point out correct form. So by way of an anti-guide, these are the cocktails that should never be consumed. Or made. Or possibly ever again be written about or even mentioned.

Orgasm, Double Orgasm, Multiple Orgasm, Frozen Orgasm . . . These horrors are all takes on the standard Orgasm (as if an orgasm could ever be described as 'standard' . . .), which combines equal parts Cointreau and Baileys. Both are liqueurs and I've got a theory that liqueurs should never be combined. The former, Cointreau, is 40 per cent alcohol grape brandy flavoured with orange peel and then sweetened; the latter is a 17 per cent alcohol Irish cream liqueur – that's Irish whisky blended with coffee-flavoured cream. Equally as revolting a drink is a B52. Built in a cocktail glass, it is one part

Mexican coffee liqueur – otherwise known as Kahlúa – one part Baileys, and one part Grand Marnier – all poured in that order, so that the different liqueurs might sit in three distinct layers. That's all the drink has to recommend it. You should just look at it, and not try to drink it.

The Brown Cow ought to scare anyone off just by its name alone. In it we have Jamaica's coffee and rum liqueur, Tia Maria, as the principal alcohol. Pour it over ice in a highball glass and then top up with milk. It's Coco Pops for sweet-toothed dipsomaniacs.

Brandy Alexanders show the true cocktail grotesqueness of that very non-co-tail ingredient, cream. Equal parts brandy, crème de cacao and cream are shaken with ice and strained into a cocktail glass. I reckon a margarita glass is a more appropriate vessel for this foul, beige-coloured thing, however, as it brings a slash of extra tastelessness to the entire event.

A Fluffy Duck (or Fluffy anything) is another creamed cocktail to be avoided. It was popular during my youth among young ladies on something called a *girl's night out*. Instead of arguing with your boyfriend on the way to the pub and then talking to your girlfriends all night, you talked to your girlfriends on the way to the pub then argued with your boyfriend once there. Fluffy Ducks seemed to help this endeavour. A shot of Advokaat mixed with a shot of Cointreau mixed with a shot of vodka and then all of this shaken over ice with a shot of milk before being strained into a highball glass and topped up with lemonade is the passport to such success. A Fluffy Duck self-administered by an emotionally unhappy young lady with a *complete dickhead* boyfriend could render said young lady legless. Often handbagless.

Even earringless. I saw Fluffy Ducks do terrible things to young girls on a number of occasions. As the Talmud tells us, 'One cup of wine is good for a woman; two are degrading; three make her wanton; four destroy her sense of shame.' One Fluffy Duck alone can take her to the fifth step . . .

The Piña Colada was similarly popular among the just-women folk. It works on a blend of light and dark rum mixed with an equal volume of pineapple juice. Coconut cream goes in, and you garnish it with a slice of pineapple and a cocktail umbrella, just to let everyone know that this drink is something only college students holidaying in Cancun should tackle. The Piña Colada makes you realise how strange young drinkers can be. If you offered them a glass of alcoholic Caribbean fish or chicken marinade to drink they'd run a mile. Some rum, some coconut cream, some pineapple juice. Leave the fish pieces in such a marinade long enough (and it doesn't take too long) and they're virtually cooked through. Marinade some chicken in it and then barbecue. The young persons would love it. The food might help line their stomach against the evils of a Piña Colada or fifty.

Next up in the evolution of young drinkers was the Cock-Sucking Cowboy. (Ideally you drink these in tandem with Double Orgasms.) Two parts butterscotch schnapps and one part Baileys. This is not really a cocktail, but a shot, or a shooter. Suitably, it uses schnapps, which is an Old Norse word meaning *to seize*. It denoted the way you drank schnapps – in one fierce swig. You float the Baileys on top of the poured schnapps using the back of a bar spoon. You order these either before you are pissed or when you are pissed, and you order them with your friends and you all drink them – I mean shoot them – in unison. You say 'Whoa-hoo!' afterwards and high-five one another. Shooters are, of course, very safe; this is because they are made in front of you on the bar and therefore they don't run the risk of anyone spiking them with rape drugs. Hell, to be doubly sure you can even buy these shooters now in pre-packed, aluminium-foil-sealed shooter glasses. They come straight out of the fridge, rendering the barman a fridge-man, or cash-registerman, rather than a fully sick, totally hot mixologist. A *CS Cowboy*, pre-packaged. Perfectly safe. Just like buying bottles of water in India with tamper-proof seals.

Speaking of things not to drink, do not drink anything made with Galliano. This liqueur was invented by a Tuscan distiller at the very end of the nineteenth century; it's an amalgam of herbs, berries, roots, and alpine flowers. There's a fair bit of anise and vanilla in it, too, judging by its smell. Judging by the taste there's also plenty of sugar. Perhaps in its most evil guise it is part-nered by sambuca and goes under a kind of tag-team wresting-show pseudonym, the Italian Stallion. Galliano, sambuca, cream: shake and strain into a cocktail glass. Just don't try any wrestling holds after drinking one of these.

And never drink (or eat) anything blue. Blue is for wearing; blue is for painting in the sky in those land-scape pictures; blue is for colourful and slightly lewd language. But blue is never for drinking. Blue Doves, Blue Ladies, Blue Lagoons, Blue Seas, Blue Hawaiians, Blue Margaritas ... They have all been tainted with the same poison: Blue Curaçao. This was originally a Dutch disaster based on white rum and bitter and under-ripe oranges from the Caribbean. The blue is just a food dye;

the flavour is still a sick-making blend of sweetness and bitterness. Perhaps this liqueur is so nasty to man because none of us can correctly pronounce its name? *Cura-say-oh, cura-kay-oh, cura-cow* . . . The word gets some shocking distortions. We mostly get the first half of the word right; but it is the *çao* that comes in for a hammering. It is, in fact, pronounced *sow*, so as to rhyme with *wow*, although as a drink it has about as much love for humanity as Chairman Mao.

All of these foul drinks do, however, serve a purpose. Only one purpose. They provide homes for those stupid little umbrellas that some people insist on sticking in mixed drinks. Some of these people are known as *flair bartenders*. They are to mixed drinks what *Disney on Ice* is to ballet. In fact, flair bartenders could probably go straight into a production of *Disney on Ice* very successfully, judging by their costumes, their cocktail-making moves – and all the ice.

The first Flair Bartending Awards I ever witnessed were held as a preamble to a big liquor industry self-funded and self-awarded awards night. Such nights see the crème de cacao of the industry's crop turn out in their gaudy finery, often dressed to some sort of fancy theme, like *Cuba!*, or *Moulin Rouge!*, or *Austin Powers!*. Yes, the themes always have exclamation marks attached. These awards hand out gongs in such categories as 'Best Packaged Light Beer On-Premise (Sales)'; or 'Most Innovative Launch of a Re-Launched Ready-to-Drink Vodka Product'. Everyone gets at least one award. Everyone networks.

The *Captain Longjohn Rum* sales team (all blonde, all women) were all wearing the same Kylie showgirl out-of-fit. In the weeks leading up to the awards night they had been practising a choreographed dance routine to perform on the open dance floor, after the awards were over and the band had started up. They are *totally awesome* and *totally amazing* and *look totally hot, and they're like totally professional dancers!* They know this. They are going to nail the dance routine just like they nail their sales budgets because they are all totally committed, self-starting sales professionals who are passionate about achieving excellence-based outcomes in an energised team environment. At least that's what the ad said for the job when they first saw it in the *Liquor Industry Monthly* magazine – a great supporter of the awards night, by the way. The magazine has a photographer there to shoot all the key advertisers, *going off on the packed dance floor!*, as the subsequent caption invariably reads. The magazine even sponsors one of the awards – usually something along the lines of 'Best Print Advertising Campaign, Pre-Mixed Rum and Cola Products (Industry Magazines)'. Or 'Best Product Launch Coverage (Industry Magazines)'. They occasionally win this one themselves. 'Amazing!' says the publisher, when accepting his own award. Everyone claps. They honestly, enthusiastically applaud. Winning your own award is seen as vital evidence – and congratulations – of liquor industry best-practice.

But to get things moving there's the flairtending pre-amble. The loosely conglomerated liquor industry – ever keen to get on board new and emerging trends, particularly when those trends involve sixteen-year-old non-consumers – are no doubt using the flairtending competition as a suck-it-and-see exercise. Who knows, if this stupid flairtending thing takes off here, well, *we grow a static sector of the on-premise market.* That is, the liquor industry sells more liquor. Spirits, liqueurs, and hideous pre-loved things in cans and bottles with porn-star-sounding names. More bars buy more of this stuff because flairtending creates a new demand. It is the same with any new, belief-beggaring sociological phenomenon. DJing created a demand for more headphones; electric leaf-blowers created a demand for longer extension leads; home-improvement TV shows created a demand for mondo grass and Grecian Blue splashbacks. None of us now could get by without these things.

But back to *Disney on Ice* – I mean the flairtending. The young men competing all had three minutes to mix three drinks, therein displaying their cocktail-making knowledge and skill – and their flair. They all looked heavily and possibly artificially suntanned, but we were in Sydney. They all had very white teeth, and used them extensively when smiling. Constantly smiling. And they all – with one exception – wore weird costumes that reminded me of pantomimes, or, yes, *Disney on Ice.* The exception was a tall and fairly lithe young man wearing black trousers and black braces over a white singlet. Oh, he also had a white sweatband around one wrist. No, hang on, isn't he the narrator in *Disney on Ice*?

As the awards-night crowd gathered in the foyers, sipping on sponsored new or test products, the competitors were introduced. They were mostly self-described mixologists; they nearly all had mixology tags, or names like Troy 'The Maestro' Khong, or Kane 'Cool McCool' Kopolopovich. They were bar managers or bartenders at the hottest shrines to mixology – Atrium, BadFur, The

Vault, The Vault 2. They had signature drinks for which they were famous. Like the Appletini Alchemist or the Feng Shui Dream. They had travelled to Germany and been a runner-up in that country's Bacardi Black Flair Cup; they were keen DJs and kite-boarders and all seemed to ride classic motorcycles. They were invariably adrenalin junkies. Bungee jumping, however, *was so, like, nineties.*

They greeted their audience with the confidence and posture of a professional dancer about to go into their routine – a routine complete with a lights show, backing music, and a voice-over commentator describing the drinks being made. Or do I mean being flaired.

McCool kicked off. He was wearing headphones. Not only was he going to flair three drinks in three minutes but he was also going to spin his twin DJ decks – or record players, as they were once called – as he did it. He started with a serious look as he dangerously counted in his opening piece of recorded music; as a violent, militaristic beat took over the foyer his expression changed from that of a surgeon to that of a cheeky schoolboy. His hands suddenly started juggling three bottles of white spirits. He'd keep two in the air as he free-poured the third one from about half a metre above the cocktail shaker. He'd glance up at the audience every few seconds, his look now changing to one of a drug dealer rather than a naughty schoolboy. Once in the open shaker the ingredients were enclosed by a large glass. He knocked the two pieces of equipment together, shook, then rolled the shaker down the back of his raised arm, Harlem Globetrotters style, across the bridge that was the back of his neck. It then went up the length of the other raised arm. He did this twice, swinging his lower body from side to side to articulate the movement of the loaded shaker on his wing-like arms. He hit the DJ deck again and checked the mix on the earphones before throwing pieces of fruit into a vitamiser, about two metres away. Every piece landed in the vitamiser. Maybe he should have been a basketball player? He set up a Martini glass on the show-bar; he set up a Margarita glass on the show bar; he poured the two drinks he'd so far fixed into each glass. Then, with only a second to go, he took out his lighter. He struck it once and let it burn. It was a long, blue flame. He free-poured whisky into a tall beer pitcher and then poured boiling water from a kettle into another; he lit the whisky and dropped the lighter and threw the boiling water from its glass into the whisky glass and back and forth. It was pyrotechnics; it was a fireworks show with a flair bartender lighting the fuse. Blue flame seemed to jerk back and forth from the two glasses, McCool acting as its artistic director. It was quite spectacular. And it was the oldest trick in the book. The other competitors did similarly Disney routines, but none of them had the big-screen firepower of McCool. He won easily.

And he'd done it by making a Blue Blazer – one of many drinks popularised by the man behind the Martinez, Professor Jerry Thomas. His display certainly drew in the crowds. It was the cocktail equivalent to Greek fire. It was finished with some sugar and a wedge of lemon, served in a shot glass. Burnt, watered-down whisky, sugared and faintly acidified. I've never tasted one. And I'll certainly never try to make one. No one should. It is to co-tails what a packet of matches is to an arsonist. Another wrong drink; another burnt-out building. Legendary, but best left in the past.

On the other hand, there are a handful of co-tails that are immutably correct, and perfect, and right; and they exist unfazed as their tastes are exquisitely unfathomable, inhabiting a world romantically remote and beyond any drinker's touch – or spoilage. These are the co-tail immortals; the drinks that never tarnish or lose lustre; drinks that deserve sacrifice and serious money. And if you don't believe me, then explain this: what other drink could possibly make anyone – whether they are a young and emotionally repressed early twentieth century Prohibition American or not – dance the Charleston? Only a co-tail could do that. Proper co-tails.

The most correct co-tail is, as we've already been told a few pages back, the Martini. I even believe that one myself. Like all true co-tails, the Martini really isn't a drink, but more of an appetiser. One or two such co-tails before dinner and the tone, timing, mood, and atmosphere of the evening is – without any apparency or obviousness – suddenly, too truly, perfect. Co-tails followed by food and wine – and accompanied by conversation – guarantees that the night takes on a calm timelessness. This can only work, of course, if you do nothing but drink your co-tail during pre-dinner co-tails. If you go to all the bother of making a perfect daiquiri and then only proceed to insult it – and your guests – by trying to drink it and prepare the salad or frig with the prawns on the grill then you are only going to get one thing out of the drink: a hangover. The idea of these drinks is to let them pass over you with no other interruptions or distractions. Once co-tailed, you'll be ready to take on dinner with your intellectual and moral compass all steady and ready to go. A couple of Martinis before the last-minute cooking and the sitting down to dinner transports you – or *co-tails* you – beyond any nervousness or tension, beyond any of those ever-present, vaguely irksome worries of the disappearing day.

In all of these drinks simplicity is the key; emphasis therefore falls to preparation and careful forethought, not stupid new ingredients or flair bartending. Which is why barmen worth their salt make their money. Whenever I see a barman really seriously yet simply fixing a drink, I know that I am in an essentially safe harbour. There's no fear when you've got a proper barman. I find respite when a proper drink is being properly made; the unknown worry that I always feel seems to momentarily subside. The drinks too soon pass, however, and the worry returns. But I'll beat it one day. I might even work out what it is. Thank goodness that in the meantime I've got a few drinks to fall back on; a few drinks that always manage to either stoke or douse the fire, depending on the need.

Here, then, is the list: ten essential co-tails. There's no particular order, but, obviously enough, the Martini is the team captain.

Martini. Gin and vermouth; for pre-dinner drinks; best made at home.

Perfect Manhattan. Good rye whisky or bourbon mixed with dry and sweet vermouth. A maraschino cherry, or a strip of orange zest. Order one in your favourite, perfect bar. Drink these alone.

Daiquiri. White rum and lime juice, with a touch of sugar syrup to bring them together. It needs to be as cold as you can get it without actually freezing. Never to be drunk while wearing long sleeves.

Brandy Sidecar. Only to be drunk while wearing long sleeves; and possibly a jacket. Brandy, Cointreau, lemon juice. Shaken. A co-tail glass. Best taken as evening light fades in the middle of winter.

Bloody Mary. Breakfast. Or a non-Spanish form of alcoholic gazpacho taken immediately before luncheon.

Long Island Iced Tea. Vodka, gin, tequila, white rum, lemon juice, ice, tall glass, top up with cola. Vicars beware. Only drink these once a year.

Singapore Sling. Shake the heck out of some ice, gin, sugar, and lemon juice. Pour over ice cubes in a tall glass and fill up with some fizzy mineral water. Float a little bit of cherry brandy on top. Garnish with a half-slice of orange. Drink these only during daylight hours and only when the humidity is over 75 per cent, preferably in the company of people you don't know too well, or might never see again.

Negroni. The perfect pick-me-up and fastest short drink in the world. Very good for drinking in crowded rooms (or bars), particularly if you're nervous or trying to pick up. Gin, Campari, sweet vermouth shaken and poured into a short glass over ice. Three at a bare minimum.

Mojito. For muddlers. So you'll need a muddling stick, and mint, and a sugar cube, and golden rum, and a touch of soda water, and a short glass and some ice. Only drink during summer and when drinking with smokers. True. Try it.

Margarita. Rim a co-tail glass with lime juice and salt; mix tequila and Cointreau. It's a party all by itself.

But not the Cosmopolitan. For obvious reasons.

Where it was once a stylish-enough drink, it has been ruined by fame. It's now the drink of cashed-up lady bogans. Nor is the Mai Tai on the list. Trouble is, it's got too many ponceforth ingredients: grenadine, curaçao, orgeat syrup . . . And the Harvey Wallbanger is a Screwdriver with Galliano on top. A Screwdriver is a waste of vodka and orange juice – a bit like a Black Velvet is a waste of champagne and Guinness.

Of course, a good Champagne Cocktail should never be sniffed at. A sugar cube doused with Grand Marnier and dropped into the bottom of a champagne flute, then drowned with good champagne. A Pink Gin. A Rolls-Royce – these are all very simple co-tails that I'd happily drink.

The key to any of them is the respect they are paid, both in preparation and in drinking. It really is like putting on a co-tail dress, or dinner suet, depending on your gender specifics or orientation. Getting dressed up means that you are up for it. You behave differently: both badly and well. The co-tail is the liquid lore of this black-tie mentality. But co-tails are not the only way to get the party started . . .

Tequila is my tragic flaw. It is my one great exception. It is like liquid cocaine. Give the assembled crowd a hit of tequila first off and some of them go crazy-crazy person. I know I do. Men who cannot dance do; and women who wear cashmere suddenly take it off. I mean disrobe. No, actually, I mean they take it off.

This is why tequila is fantastically evil and mind-altering. The key to its effect does not lie in agave cacti or in alcohol-preserved worms. Like a Martini's metaphysical side, tequila has a strange power of personality. It out-thinks you, in the manner of a Jedi knight, plays with your mind – to the point where you dance when you can't and remove your cashmere sweaters when you shouldn't. I know it is mentally superior to us because I ran a test. The only thing I can't believe is that the *British Medical Journal* keeps turning my results down for publication.

There's a back story, of course. There's always a back story.

I was in a high-powered meeting with an editrix. We were getting on it very mildly at luncheon, drinking white wine and rosé and having a giggle. Talk ran to white spirits and what they do to you – and which ones you can tolerate, and which ones you – for some strange reason – can't. The editrix mentioned tequila. I gender-biasedly assumed she was going to say that tequila did horrible things to her; knowing as I know with so much certainty that some drinks are not drinks for ladies. But she liked tequila, and she drank it to get her dinner parties going. 'It's fantastic; it's more like a drug than a drink.'

Apparently – at these dinner parties – before everyone partook of the tapas-style canapés or sat down to shredded duck and sesame-seed seaweed salad they had some tequila. Shot glasses. There were no rules. You could shoot it, slam it, sip it, drink half of it and then add some lime juice or lemonade – it didn't matter. But every-one had to have a tequila before they got anything else to drink or anything to eat. 'They're always the best dinner parties . . .' she said.

This was something that I was clearly going to have to run through the lab. Tequila-inspired dinner parties where the talk is always boisterous yet happy – and, according to the report – also witty . . . Well, this hardly fitted the commonly held notion of tequila, um, appreciation. Kids not yet twenty lick, suck, and slam the stuff; thirty-somethings don't drink tequila.

Two experiments were set up. I'd hold two dinner parties for eight people three weeks apart. Why eight people and why three weeks apart can be explained by numerologists. When conducting scientific research, the number eight – when applied to patients – guarantees the most reliable results. The number three – where time is concerned – ensures unquestionable, even outcomes. You shouldn't dream of running an experiment like this without the strictest adherence to science's fullest rigour.

Both dinner parties were made up of a broad mix of humanity. Adult specimens, male and female. All drank to varying degrees of satisfaction. None were pregnant, none were 'no-thanks-I'm-driving', none were sick. None were obviously drunk on arrival. Speaking of which . . .

The first dinner party, DP–A, started off with champagne. Proper, expensive champagne. Three bottles of it. (There's that number three again . . .) Hilary had on her cranky face; she was cranky with Nick, who was not doing what she wanted him to do all the time. Peter might have had a few at lunchtime; it was a Friday night, so I suppose you could expect a few people to have had a *business meeting* during the course of the day. Greg and Tania were busy talking about Greg's new CV for the new job he was going to get, and Helen was full of exciting news about a fantastic seminar she had been to on *Multicultural Australian Health Issues among Migrant Women – Current Thinking*. It was about halfway through the main course before the champagne and white wine platform upon which the night had thus far been built came into proper effect. Conversation turned to gentle ribbing, reminiscence, safe gossip, our Nicole and Keith, that sort of thing. The evening ticked over like one of those hybrid electric cars – sensibly, sedately, environmentally. People thanked me for a wonderful night. People ordered cabs or rode bicycles home. It was a perfectly pleasant dinner party. Yes, quite torturous. It made me want to sleep. In a way, I had been sleeping – all through the night. The robotic march of dinner and conversation was so automated that I felt I could've done the whole thing as a zombie.

Which leads us to DP–B. Same conditions; same sort of *nice* people. But not champagne. No. Not $240 worth of fine French sparkling wine. Just $35 worth of cheap tequila. Oh, and eight shot glasses. I bought them from the $2 shop. They were $2.50 each. Oh, and I bought some limes, too. They were even more expensive than the shot glasses.

Some guests seemed a little perturbed about tackling the tequila. Shot glasses can have that effect on certain personalities. The little glass pricks some deep psychological fear or some sort of buried trauma. Syringes can have a similar effect, which is probably a good thing, though – otherwise we might all be on heroin. I explained the new rule. No drinks and no dinner until everyone has had their Mexican medicine. Trev downed his shot in one go and asked for another one. He yelped like a rodeo clown and even used a weird accent when he commented on how good tequila makes you feel. He had just come off the end of a seven-year up and down, on and off relationship with his girlfriend, however. She was now known as the Seven-Year Bitch. Rebecca slammed her tequila down rather too professionally. She turned to Cynthia and said, in a little girl's voice, 'Uh-oh. I sink Wubecca is going to be bad tonight . . .' Cynthia almost sucked the inside of the shot glass dry and asked, 'Can I have something posh to drink now, and lots of it?'

Rob was the only one showing any signs of reluctance. 'I know what this stuff can do to you . . .' he said, as I gave him something of a suspicious eye. I'd just slammed my second shot, though, so maybe I was trying to get my vision back to twenty-twenty. Rebecca and Cynthia had found the corkscrew and were now opening all the wine. All of it. I pulled two pizzas out of the oven and the sophisticated finger food began. Rob had nowhere to hide, so he did the right thing. But it took him two goes to get the stuff down. Pizza turned into some sort of fish dish that then became a mixed barbecue. And the neighbours came in late because they figured it was better to join the party than listen to it, and I think Trev went home with Cynthia, but only after they'd left a karaoke bar in town at 2 am. They are still friends; probably because neither of them really remember too much of what did or didn't happen. And, strangely enough, I didn't feel all that good in the morning. Nor all that bad, either.

This sort of shameless tequila-fuelled behaviour is all fine and good when you do it in the privacy of your own home, in the company of trust-ish-worthy friends. Behaving in such a way at an office party is not so wise, however, which is why the following advice might be useful for some younger persons.

Drinking at work, otherwise known as an office party, can be extremely unwise. Whether it be a barbecue in a local park, a banqueting room of a cheap Chinese restaurant, or some finger food and frothies in the staff canteen, some of us can come an awful cropper at such events as, say, the annual office Christmas party. If you get the drinking wrong at this time of year there might not be a job to come back to after New Year. Having been sacked on more than one occasion for being drunk, I've got some thoughts on the matter, and on Christmas work parties in general.

No, no, no: I am not going to start by saying those lame things like 'drink responsibly, eat food, have a glass of water every second drink . . .' Good and sensible advice this might be, BUT NO ONE DOES IT. So if you reckon you might get on it and be silly at the party, try these realistic and practical protocols instead.

Get in a school. Drink at the same rate and disposition as a few other people you work with. This means that if anything goes wrong the blame is shared. They might sack one drunken idiot but they won't sack four of you. Then again . . .

Preparation is a four-step procedure: have your mobile phone charged, leave your credit cards at home, take $100 in cash, and wear the work shirt and tie you hate most. This sort of planning means that if things become pear-shaped you will still be able to ring a cab, you'll not blow (or lose) the credit card, and, well, the shirt and tie do not matter. What I like about this plan the most is the way it invariably guarantees a quiet, safe and enjoyable night. Let's face it: the only time you end up in the back of a police car is when a) the mobile is dead; b) the credit card is lost; c) the $250 shirt is ripped and d) the Italian silk tie is covered in Frangelico. It is a sort of reverse Murphy's Law at work here.

Don't play any sort of sport at office Christmas parties. Ping-pong, touch rugby, badminton, carpet bowls, darts – definitely not darts. I don't think this rule needs any explanation. Drinking and dud sportsmen do not mix.

Don't talk to anyone who is not a member of your own sex. This means that you will not discover – just after you've asked her out – that the hot chick in admin is a lesbian in a loving relationship. It also means that your various female superiors will continue to think that you are a lovable larrikin who prefers to hang around with the boys. Office parties are the worst possible time for any essentially unemployable and talentless man to appear on any lady superior's HR radar.

Drink beer or wine. But not both. And do not under any circumstances drink whisky, bourbon or rum at a work Christmas bash. Unless you are a tow-truck driver or a Harley-Davidson mechanic. Then you can do whatever you like. There is one drink, however, that even a tow-truck-driving Harley-Davidson rider with an Olympic liver would struggle to defeat. Sparkling shiraz. It seems initially appealing and 'fun'. Sparkling shiraz is about as Christmasly festive as you can get. It is a uniquely Australian drink and has the added advantage of being a very appropriate beverage to consume with ham or turkey. Blokes like it because it has shiraz in it; girls like it because it has bubbles in it. And when drunk in gender-unison it usually leads to some late-night karaoke or dancing, after which anything can happen, maybe even with the hot lesbian admin chick in that formerly loving relationship. But one too many units of sparkling shiraz and it can be all over red rover. And regurgitated fizzy red can be all over quite a number of things. To borrow from the advice of Sir Les Patterson, forget the dry cleaners, you might be best to burn the suit.

5

Getting your beerjo back

You can't be a real country unless you have a beer and an airline – it helps if you have some kind of football team or some nuclear weapons, but at the very least you need a beer.
– Frank Zappa

It came on without any warning and with no formal announcement. It occurred as if some sort of random act; there was no rhyme or reason; there was no explanation and no rationale. I felt like a lonely and helpless victim of a cruel and remorseless disease. I'd lost my beerjo.

It happened in the worst possible place at the worst possible time – as seems to befit this medical condition's particularly nasty and virulent pathology. It happened in the pub at the end of a long working day, at approximately 2.45 pm. I was unprepared; there was no professional help available, and as far as I knew my health insurance didn't stretch to this sort of cover. I was bereft, or possibly even beereft.

A business colleague was at the bar; he'd just ordered

a beer. He leant against the bar of the pub as if the bar –
and, indeed, the entire pub – had been built around him.
The bar and the man formed a kind of cantilever effect:
the one without the other might cause the whole place to
tip over on its architectural arse. The business colleague
was not only acting in an engineering capacity, however;
he was multi-tasking. Unsatisfied by merely propping
up the bar (and the building), he was also holding a ten-
dollar bill. I caught his eye as I swung around the corner
of the bar; his eye immediately caught the eye of the
barmaid, and with a twist and dip of the head he silently
adjusted his order from one beer to two. That's when
something went snap inside my main beer processing
centre. It wasn't like a fan belt had broken but more like
all the fan belts, pulleys, wheels and runners had been
entirely removed from the engine bay. I pressed the
beer accelerator and absolutely – *completely* – nothing
happened. I'd lost my beerjo; it had left the building.

There was nowhere to run to, baby, and nowhere to
hide. Like some poof, gourmet wanker I stood at the bar
not drinking my beer. I never want to feel that way again.
But, quite frankly, getting through it, coming out the
other side, alive and in love with beer (and life) again,
well, it makes chemotherapy look like a cheap haircut.
Which, in a way, it sort of is; but you know what I mean.

I took advice.

'What? You're off beer?' This is how one treasured
colleague responded. 'Fuck . . .'

'You can't drink beer any more? Jesus, have you
become a girl or something?' That was another caring
word or two.

'Always knew you were a wine faggot . . .' whispered
another mate. Ex-mate.

Having consulted the professionals I decided that the only way to beat this disease was to tackle it head on, all on my own. I would go to the edge of oblivion and stare into the crevice that fell immeasurably below; and I would walk away stronger, with truth and knowing; and – hopefully – a really fucking big thirst.

So I moved into a pub. Here beer could not avoid me, nor me it. Only one of us would emerge victorious. Only one of us would get out alive.

The Upton Arms is a small two-storey pub on a corner, built in 1927. It's retro-daggy, with too many customers sporting tattoos and hairdon'ts and retro clothes and all smoking and drinking cheap pots of semi-cold beer. There's a front bar that is always hidden in a cloud of said smoke. There's a beer garden where the barely aged and the casual customers mingle, while smoking and drinking and laughing hysterically at what Lach did last Saturday night when he'd taken an ecky on top of a Red Bull and vodka. In between there's a DJ's booth with two decks and two boxes of truly awful records that the team of ninety-three DJs all constantly remove and reload while holding one half of a headphone set to one ear while smoking and talking to the other ninety-two DJs about how so completely they are not being seen to be DJing. Opposite the front bar, behind the service area, is a ladies' lounge, behind which runs the dining room and kitchen. Everything is old brown paint and dis-tressed carpet and half-arsed 1930s wainscoting. Some of the light-fittings work; some of the staff work; none of the customers do – but they still hand over the readies for the beer and the shooters and the odd bottle of *woine*. I'd been drinking in this pub for about two years. I'd ended up here because the rest of my postcode had become too Benetton. All the pubs and bars had been bought up by conglomerates and brewers and wankers and nightclub millionaires. All the old joints had been turned into lifestyle venues and coffee franchises and pizza-slice depots and fashion stores. This meant there was nowhere left for a dishonest man to honestly drink. Except the Upton Arms. It was a little bit out of the way, and a little bit hard to get to, and a little bit hard to park at, and a little bit imbued with attitude.

The door policy, for instance.

Due to the continuing rise in antisocial behaviour we are compelled to enforce some new door policies and explain a couple of old ones:

NEW: No suits and no collars up.
OLD: No Bucks, Hens or Pub Crawls
OLD: NO Team 'Colours'
Not for any sport . . . not even AFL

Yes it is Victoria and yes we all have a team but the Upton Arms bears no favour nor malice. We leave our allegiances at the door and we appreciate that you will do the same.

Under no circumstances is alcohol to be brought into or removed from the premises . . . it is simply the Law.

Please drink responsibly and be considerate of others.

If you can't exercise self-control, we will.

Please respect us and our venue and we will respect you.

Enjoy your evening.

Much of the reasoning – if that's what you can call it – behind this innovative piece of creative sociology came from the manager. He was affectionately known by the staff as 'Senior Management'. He was always easy to pick, because he had a wobbly head. He was a mid-thirties hospitality-industry professional; he was a part-time DJ; part-time motorcycle racer; part-time tattoo expert; and occasional-time bar manager. More importantly, his favourite number was '6'. Everyone knew this because '6' was plastered on his motorcycle helmet, his laptop, his DJ deck, his motorcycle's petrol tank, his leather jacket, and possibly even his dick. The wobbly head was his way of being too-cool-for-school. It wasn't that there was anything mechanically wrong with his head, but it had the swagger of Rick James's entire body. He coupled the wobbly head with a few other moves. His right index finger was invariably pointing at you in the shape of a gun; his left arm was invariably swinging across the front of his body, affecting some sort of disco or dance move completed by a click of the fingers or a 'hot' word from the wobbly head's lips. He always walked away from you backwards. He always had a new shaving mistake. Moustaches, beards. Beards, moustaches. Long hair, no hair, someone else's hair. His entire shift was consumed by baseball-cap wardrobe changes. When he dealt with customers the customers were told they were wrong, in the wrong place, not welcome, or that they actually didn't want the drink they had ordered because Wobbly Head knew what they *needed*. 'That's why they pay me the big bucks . . .' he would add. Ugly young bogan Greek girls would occasionally find this behaviour attractive and laugh and giggle. He'd serve them their drink and ask them a question about what the word 'vodka' actually meant and when one of them would say, 'Oh, I don't know. Is it "horny"!?' he'd point his pistol finger at her and reply, 'That's why I'm gonna go out with YOU!' They'd all giggle and laugh again. And keep buying vodka.

Into this I moved. Moved in. A wastrel with a beer problem.

I shouldn't suppose it is ever a really good time to move into a pub. Then again, can it ever be a *bad* time? Losing your beerjo doesn't help. Nor do other emotional issues.

It was a Monday night. Monday night after dinner. Apparently well after dinner. Too after dinner for one other member of personnel. 'Enjoy your life!' was what I think she said when I announced my pub-moving-into-beerjo-saving plan. It was a fair enough comment. It was her place. For one brief moment I was a drummer. You know the joke about drummers. What do you call a drummer without a girlfriend? Homeless . . .

Drummers always go to the pub. I did too, but I lived there.

There was a room there – temporarily vacated by the Assistant Lady Bar Manager, currently on house-sitting leave for a former cashed-up ex-non-reformed-lesbian lover.

Time for a deep breath.

It was early winter. I had with me a laptop computer, a pen, a notepad, and a case of red wine. Oh, and also some clothes and a white bed sheet. The white bed sheet was a last-minute inclusion to my touring party; I don't know why it was included; maybe I got the jitters.

Upstairs at the Upton Arms lay a broken conglomerate of rooms – some private bedrooms, one an office, another a type of common room full of dysfunctional TVs, skiing equipment, DJ turntables and motorcycle parts. All it lacked was a snow machine and some girls in bikinis wearing Ugg boots. There was a kitchen too, but that's another story. A horror story.

One of the private rooms had a big 'D' on the door. It didn't stand for door. And nor did the door: it didn't lock. The 'D' stood for Diana, the Assistant Lady Bar Manager who was letting me have the room. Being a door in a red early-twentieth-century double-brick building, it and its room had the ingrained feel and sense of an earlier and certainly more desperate time and place. A hopeless man could have felt determinedly suicidal in such a room fifty years earlier, but it was now double-brick comfort and respectability to me. Despite the nude art photographs.

Diana, the Assistant Lady Bar Manager, was an actress. She wasn't glamorous nor was she trite. She had natural beauty. She had the sort of confidence and ease of relaxed posture only found in young women who have themselves shot in naked portraiture.

The two mounted photographs were the first two pieces of alteration to the room. I'm not a prissy conservative. And I'm not repressed (he said . . .). But I was moving into a pub and I was moving into a room hitherto inhabited by an attractive girl whose creative and artistic impulses were evidenced by two 8×6 black and whites. They had to go.

The jitters soon faded, however. Moving into a pub to – ostensibly – repair my beerjo and also to write silly stories for magazines, I was greeted on my first night with the annual staff party. I was invited because I lived at the pub. The party was *at* the pub. Upstairs. Not in my room but next to it. It started at 10 pm and was aided by all the leftover and unsold pre-mixed vodka and orange cans from the last stocktake. And a karaoke machine. And the world's worst wireless microphone.

We promptly got on it. Not the microphone, but the drink.

The drink helped the karaoke. About twenty members of this strange ship's inventory gathered around it. They all rowed in unison – to the sound of a badly timed, spastic karaoke metronome. The Japanese have more to apologise for than the war and whaling and hubcap platters full of pre-loved sushi. Honestly, people couldn't be more out of tune if they tried. They could wrap a hungry boa constrictor around their necks and stick an elderly footballer's sock down their throat and still sound better.

Of course, by this stage I'd sung a bad version of Glen Campbell's 'Rhinestone Cowboy' and I'd had a few. And a few other things. The entire effect was to make me say and do things I will never regret but never purposefully remember. Unless I hear certain songs again.

It was an odd mixture of a night though. I was a regular who was suddenly a resident; yet I was partying with the staff . . . As much as the staff of any pub – or the crew, as they term themselves – must hate the way regular customers every night so slowly and then suddenly more quickly deteriorate under the J-curve effects of assured alcohol consumption, customers can readily bridle before the free and Dionysian performance of unleashed bar staff. Me; them; the karaoke; the free grog. It seemed sort of not quite right. But I was three-quarters drunk and half-interested. Particularly in the way the children performed.

Because they were all children. Even the mid-thirties wobbly head was a twelve-year-old. It showed in the way they danced. Or didn't. Top Hat drum tsssks were mimicked by flicks of fingers and hands. The boys danced every beat on the top symbol strike, never on the bass beat. Everyone was a lead singer, or a lead guitarist, or a diva, or all three. Maybe the bad booze was to blame. We were certainly well-fuelled. E, after all, does equal MC squared. Or, rather, badly pissed behaviour requires a mixture of crap drinks. Pity Einstein wasn't a barman. We'd now have no nukes, just civilisation-flattening daiquiris. The Iranians wouldn't be destroying Israel with dirty warheads, but with coffee and saffron-infused 100-proof alcopops.

Yep, they were all children; and all children running a pub. But they were mostly good children; they liked to drink and they didn't do too many bad drugs. They were tolerant of all forms of sexuality and perhaps because of that they didn't seem to have any sexual hang-ups. They talked frankly to their mums about what they'd been up to. They hadn't let any one form of music tribalise them; they were keen surfers but didn't drown in surf's jargon or nihilistic anti-ambition. They all worked and they didn't steal anything from one another – not even each other's food out of the fridge. Speaking of which, that's where I went; not to steal, but to redistribute. The staff fridge had a loaf of some sort of women's health-soy-anti-gluten bread in it, and a block of rat-trap cheese, and a half-eaten avocado. There was also a tub of pretend butter, its claim to nutritional fame being that it was 'spreadable'. Two frypans were turned into a toasted sandwich machine and I became the 2 am caterer.

Cooking for people is always much more fun when you've been on it, and they are still on it. And it is better to fry cheese and avocado sandwiches than it is to sing karaoke. But among all of this I still couldn't find my beerjo. The vodka and orange drinks and some bad wine had made me feel a little uninhibited, but there was as yet no taste for beer. The final song of the night was Jimmy Hendrix's guitar solo of 'The Star-Spangled Banner'. The wobbly head did some karaoke air guitar to it. It remains among one of the best and at the same time worst visual experiences of my life.

The empty, quiet early morning was the most peculiar time to be in a pub. There were the ghosts, and the crisp, long, clearly demarcated shadows made from the day's first light. And there was the sense of all of those millions of drinks. In the early hours the Upton Arms was like a long-silent battleground; it was the pub equivalent to the beaches of Gallipoli on a cold winter's morning. There was a sense of the supernatural. All those dead drinks, all killed for no reason. Smells of carpets and bar-top runners; temporarily sleeping deep-fryers; the fug of cigarettes past – all mingling with the thoughts of a very vaguely destitute pub devotee dressed in twenty-four-hour denim. The ghosts didn't scare me; indeed, I was hoping they might lead me to the other side, back to beer. And just as I was imagining they were about to communicate to me, just as their presence began to feel all too real, the cleaner banged open the side door. Reality descended with a lightning-fast thud. I felt like strangling the cleaner. Never scare a beer ghost. Friends couldn't help me. A party didn't get me back on the frothies; and now beer in its supernatural guise had vanished wispily, perhaps for ever. It was therefore time to get some religion.

I turned to a Trappist monk. His name was Chimay. Bottle-conditioned Belgian Trappist monk-brewed ale at 9 per cent alcohol by volume and 330 millilitres in total. He had a crown seal and a vintage year – 2002. He'd been sitting in my office's 'cellar' for about three years. He was the direct connection to a passionate, beer-brewing Christ. He was made in Belgium under the supervision of monks, who had made him since 1862, and whose tradition went back to the end of the Roman Empire, and, before that, into the bleary-eyed past of the earliest European maltsters and brewers. Ale. Ale was Adam to the beer-drinking world. Ale begat lager, from his rib, and that was Eve. Easy. Seductive. But not ale. Chimay channelled the thousands of years of ale's weight and girth and worth and merit. And it's holy blessing. This beer was my Holy Grail. And my salvation.

It was a tiny little dump bottle. Dark brown in colour, sporting a very simple and vaguely post-medieval label. *Chimay. Pères Trappistes.* Being a vintage beer meant it was a Christmas beer, or so it had been in tradition. The strongest alcohol and the most complex beer the Chimay brewery/monastery makes. Like any bottle-conditioned ale it likes to think about things in a cellar for a while, letting all the flavours and components meld and integrate. Like some wine can do. Chimay comes from the Abbaye Notre-Dame de Scourmont, close to the town of Chimay itself. The abbey's wells provide the water for the beer, and the abbey's walls still circle the working brewery, although the brewery work is now conducted by lay people, under the monk's ale-charged supervision. But monks and beer?

Yes, monks and beer. Beer is to Belgium what wine is to France. Enter any Belgian restaurant or café and the beer list will easily outweigh the wine one. And as you are deciding which beer to try, the Rubenesque waitress plonks a bowl of cheese on the table, with a bowl of mustard. Toothpicks stab the cheese and cheese goes into mustard. Beer – beer of any description – is then instantly necessary and fabulous. But the Belgians know something about this game.

At the turn of the twentieth century, Belgium – a tiny country – had 3000 working breweries. They produced beers as broad and as wide-ranging as wild yeast lambics, fruit beers, wheat beer, lush and rich cherry beer, brown beer, red beer, and saison . . . Many of these beers are as old and as untrendy as anything you can imagine. With no regard for low carbohydrates or low alcohol, brewers in Belgium continue to do that which they do so well. Lambic beer is a good case in point – for lambic brewing is something few – hang on – *no* commercial brewers would try to make anywhere else in the world. Wild yeasts living and migrating from bits of brewery equipment and brewery architecture float about when the time is right, landing themselves in the vats of pregnant beer. This was the way fruits and sugars used to ferment. It was, before any chemical understanding of the process was developed, considered divine. As if by magic, water and malt would brew. They would ferment and then they would stop. And the resultant liquid was life-giving, and spicy, and tart, and refreshing, and alcoholic. I mean mind-improving. But this was a world away, in a medieval past, where there were no seatbelts and no breathalysers. Just monks making beer. A world away. Nowadays lady vicars can't even talk about God for fear of offending a minority group.

Chimay did not always find favour with the Lord, however. Following World War II things fell apart and the centre looked like it wouldn't hold. But God sent a Belgian chemist to help. Professor Jean De Clerck from Leuven University helped the monks develop their own very unique yeast strain. This yeast would put Chimay back on the beer map. Control and steady supply, a good source of water, ample grain for malt; and a unique yeast strain. Chimay prospered, and when the chemist died in the late 1970s he was buried in the abbey.

This beer would surely save me.

Being winter and being a person that doesn't mind a bit of cold weather there was no reason for me to chill the Chimay at the office. It came out of the cupboard – I'm sorry, *the cellar* – and stood up on the tasting bench for half an hour. I don't know why I felt it had to stand up for half an hour, but it seemed like the right thing to do at the time. Chimay stubbies look like solid and immutable things. They have an assured but by no means arrogant presence. They look like the beer *is*. Like something that is trustworthy and like something that is old-fashioned. Bigger, 750 millilitre versions of this beer even come with a champagne-style cork stopper, which makes them look even more old-school posh. Unfortunately, the only time I have tried such a version of Chimay the cork had imparted some taint into the beer. Yes, corked beer.

But this little bottle had a crown seal and was doing what only a handful of people can do in the world with any degree of positive and pleasurable effect. It was wearing brown on blue. Apparently, they should never meet; but the blue label and the brown bottle smacked of a time well before fashion. Besides, you don't tell a monk how to dress. I opened the bottle and poured it out in one even, flowing motion into a large wine glass. Belgian beer glasses are more often than not closer to wine glasses than the unimaginative glass vessels that dominate Australian and English beer service. So a wine glass was necessary for a monk's beer. It's a dark ale that runs the gamut of cocoa to blackcurrant to smokiness and beyond. Its headiness is entirely matched by its richness and its silky, long, pure texture. It's more like a hedonist's breakfast than it is beer; but this is to misunderstand what such ales are all about. They are not just for drinking. They are for living on, and off, and from. One of these beers can keep you going all night.

All I needed it to do was jump-start my beerjo. All I needed it to do was to clear my mind of all the doubts and all the beereftness. I needed to find a place where, mentally, I could wipe the disc clean and then re-install the beer program. If I could enter into such a trancelike state then I knew my hand would involuntarily reach for the Trappists' Beercharist and I would be ready to get to the pub again. To drink from the well in a proper fashion.

I tried to think pure thoughts. Barley. Malt. Pure, clean water. Wild yeasts. Perfect hop flower-heads full of oil; perfect hop heads that are only one or two botanical steps away from cannabis. I'm not sure if I said 'Om', but the next thing I knew I was drinking from the Lord's wine glass; then, via a Trappist monk's grace, I felt the power of beer fall upon me. Long, life-giving, powerful ale ran through my body and through my veins like a miracle cure from a fire-and-brimstone Baptist Bible Belting Basher's outstretched healing hand. Praise the Lord. I went straight to the pub. I felt cured. I could drink beer again.

Straight to the pub. But the closer I got, the more a sense of minor trepidation grew. The monk Chimay had done something for me, but would his blessing translate into sessional drinking? This was make or break time. It was either beer for ever or beer never again.

Through the front double door. Through the front double doors so narrow you had to open both of them to get in. Past the front bar, head down, not looking at any of the locals or any of the cigarette smoke or the two reasonably attractive women sitting at the corner of the bar. OK, maybe I did look at them for a second. Through the nook and past the service counter and into the back bar, or ladies' lounge, where I invariably drank.

And then the Lord worked once again in a mysterious way.

Tommy the barman stood before me, behind the bar, both hands on the beer-mat runner, his *Keep On Truckin'* baseball cap fitting snugly on his head, his long moustache stretching his face further south than it really went, his T-shirt posing a badly printed rhetorical question, below which was an arrow pointing to his belt: *Well, it's not going to suck itself?* I looked at him as I reached for a $5 bill in my pocket, and as I did I said hello.

'Cuz,' he replied. He called everyone Cuz.

And then I saw it. A beer on the bar. And then Tommy

raised his hand in rejection of my $5 bill, turning his head to one side, closing his eyes in the process.

'No, Cuz, this one's on me. It's my knock-off drink; but I want you to have it, Cuz.'

It was a 375 millilitre stubby of Melbourne Bitter, icy cold, straight out of the ice and slush bucket behind the bar, where Tommy kept the coldest beer. It was Tommy's free knock-off drink, but he was selflessly offering it to me. Sacrificing his own free drinking pleasure for my well-funded and yet ultimately unearned one.

My mind sifted all of this information and all of this other-worldliness and then I noticed something truly miraculous. The stubby was suddenly empty.

'Jeez, Cuz, you got a thirst today or what?' commented Tommy, as he plonked another beer on the bar, this time taking my $5 bill.

'It must be the way you serve them, Tommy.'

Mimicking senior management, he replied, 'Well, *that's why they pay me the big bucks*, Cuz . . .'

'In fact, Tommy, you're this pub's version of a poncy restaurant's sommelier.'

'Hey, that's the dude that pours the wine and makes you taste it, yeah?'

'Yeah. They're the wine wankers. Sommeliers.'

'Maybe I could be, like, a *Beerelier*?'

'Oh no, Tommy, your powers transcend mere beereliering, believe me . . .'

'Yeah?'

'Believe me . . .'

And then the evening really began.

The regulars started furtively slipping in through the narrow double doors at the front corner of the pub. It was about 5.30 in the late afternoon, and the light of an occasionally wet winter was beginning to fade. In the muted wall-mounted lighting the pub's interior took on a warm glow; the wainscoting seemed less marked and scarred; the heliotrope wallpaper that ran above the dark timber panelling suggested a familiar, softly spoken formality. Tommy had earlier lit the fire in the ladies' lounge and with so few people in the place you could hear it crackle and occasionally snap as it threw a red-hot ember out onto the black-blood-red octogenarian carpet, complete with its little floral motifs. Whoever stood closest to the fire had to kick the ember back in. It was one of those unwritten pub rules, unlike the door policy, which was definitely written.

A few old blokes still drank at this pub's front bar, which I always consider to be a good sign. It means the publican isn't a drug-dealing nightclub millionaire determined to drag the *venue* into the twenty-first century. It shows that the publican is still interested in some small way in a sense of the local pub's community. Well, maybe. What it does show is that the publican is making enough money out of the place to not be bothered with growth, or expansion, or redevelopment, or succession plans, or future-proofing, or any of those other CPA-style business innovations. The pub is making enough money; the publican is stripping enough money out of the business. It's a leaky boat, the Upton Arms, and any architect worth his vintage Saab collection would kill to accept the brief, but then where would the locals go? And what would happen to the honest drinkers?

One of the old blokes was Jimmy. He was a retired

beer-truck driver. He had fantastic false teeth that flashed bright white light through the bar. The teeth were always on show, just below his reddish nose and cheeks and his Brylcreemed grey-black hair, combed hard and flat back over his head. No matter what the weather he always wore a thin woollen pullover atop a polo shirt. He turned up at about five o'clock most days and sipped from an old five-ounce glass that the bar staff kept for his private use. The more he drank, the closer he got to the bar, both vertically and horizontally. The more he drank the more he flashed his teeth. The more he drank the less anyone could understand his low-toned but well-paced whispering. When the bar staff couldn't understand what he was saying any more they'd cut him off. He never seemed to mind this. He'd sit for a bit longer with his empty five-ounce and smile and whisper and look at people at the bar without ever really making eye contact. And then he'd be gone.

Sitting to Jimmy's right, in pole position at the front bar, would be Mal. He was a builder. He used to be a builder. He was a developer now and did most of his building by mobile telephone, yelling into it with his thick Australian chainsaw accent, telling the builders that worked for him what to *fucking do with the fucking wall fucking unit for the fucking reno at number fifty-fucking-two in O-fucking-Brien Street. For fuck's sake, do I have to fucking well install it me-self?* Mal always wore yachting clothes, as he was a keen yachtsman who regularly re-developed houses from quite a number of nautical miles out to sea. One must assume he did this via satellite phone. Mal was also keen on car racing, but strictly from the point of view of an informed, could-have-done-it, too-old-to-do-it-now perspective. But Mal's real gift and real passion and what he loved to do as much as possible was smoke. In one drinking session he could single-handedly provide enough smoke for the Upton Arms to live on for about a week. Lighting, inhaling, exhaling, or simply holding the cigarette, Mal could make that little smouldering stick of death pump out more smoke than an MGM Indian with a large incinerator and a wet blanket. Smoke seemed to follow him like a pet dog. Smoke even seemed to appear when he bought a pack of cigarettes over the bar.

The other more regular regulars were the staff. They were the only staff ever to get to work, not just on time, but well before time. About an hour before their shift. Not only did the staff enjoy knock-off drinks, but they also enjoyed knock-on drinks. Never to excess, of course. Tommy, the beerelier, might have a beer; Mikey, the bass player, might have a cheeky stubby too; Helen, the actress, would take a pink gin; Diana, the Assistant Lady Bar Manager and also an actress, would stick to the bottled minis of Italian mineral water. (These mini bottles of expensive Italian mineral water I have never actually seen sold to an actual customer, but they remain always in stock . . .) Stuart, whose stage-pub name was Wrecker, would shotgun a Red Bull and yell and scream and go *Whoa-hoa!* before slamming a shot of Jägermeister. He would then tell the bar, the staff, and much of the local residential vicinity that he was ON DUTY AND ON FIRE AND LADIES LOOK OUT TONIGHT! WWWWWWHOA-HOA! Jonathan, whose stage name was Desperado, would very quietly have a beer or two, but it was often hard to tell with Desperado whether he was actually on duty or not. Indeed, he often worked more energetically and enthusiastically when he was in the pub on his day off. Wrecker and Desperado mostly ran the beer-garden bar, which was a kind of tikki hut affair with two beer taps and a fridge. Wrecker manned the taps and Desperado ran the glasses and ice and replacement bottles of such sophistimicated drinks as Bundaberg rum or Canadian Club whisky. Wrecker liked the division of labour. HEY DESPERADO, YOU WIENER, YOU'RE GONNA BE MY BITCH TONIGHT! It was a good thing that, deep down inside, Desperado had a sense of humour . . .

The Upton worked on a cash-only basis. There were also no credit-card facilities; this was assuaged by the presence of an automatic teller machine that never worked. It was right next to the door to the toilets, however, so at least it played a vital role as a landmark and meeting point.

A meeting point for the inner-city trendoids and try-hards that mostly made this place tick over and pay. The usual crowd wasn't made up of kids. There was no television in the Upton Arms, so, well, no 18-year-old new drinkers felt safe. The usual crowd wasn't made up of real-estate agents and insurance sales-professionals in their late thirties going through their first divorce. The Upton was too grungy and too badly serviced for this sub-section of mid-life's sexual meat market. They preferred to hang around in fully refurbished pubs like the Water Pump, a few kilometres down the road. This old boozer had been stylishly reinvigorated after a trio of footballers' wives had bought the freehold. What it once was and what it became were two entirely different things. Imagine taking the Elephant Man and changing him into Britney Spears, yet when doing so not actually changing his basic body shape. Superficial and cosmetic refubishments only. You then tell the world how fabulous the new Elephant Man looks ... This is what happens when three footballers' wives-slash-girlfriends redecorate an old working-men's hotel. This is what happens to an old pub when three such footballers' girlfriends redecorate an old hotel using nothing more than their mobile phone cameras and a couple of bottles of sauvignon blanc.

The usual crowd at the Upton wasn't made up of tradesmen, although a couple would drink in the front bar on weeknights up until about six o'clock. The crowd wasn't musicians or druggies or TV production nobodies or journos or firemen or nurses or hospitality-industry professionals. I mean waiters and waitresses. It wasn't any one of these groups of people; it was all of these things. And what meshed all of these people together to make them the half-sedated heaving mass that was the Upton's crowd on any given night was the pub's own personality. All those ghosts of dead drinks. The toilets that were never clean or flushing or lockable. The ashtrays in the beer garden that were never emptied. The beer garden that was a smoker's paradise. The half-cold tap beer. The chipped beer glasses. The old carpet. The wobbly stools and tables. The tattoos on the staff. The piercings *in* the staff. The no-credit-card policy. The cash-machine-temporarily-out-of-service policy. The door policy that wouldn't let anyone in.

I had one more beer and felt entirely refreshed. Best to get myself home. So I mis-scaled the stairs and made a toasted avocado and cheese sandwich and drank half a bottle of bad red wine and closed the door with the big 'D' on it and slept the tipsy sleep of the semi-just. My beerjo had *re-entered* the building. Amen.

119

6

How to survive a wine tasting

What is man, when you come to think upon him, but a
minutely set, ingenious machine for turning, with infinite
artfulness, wine into urine?
– Isak Dinesen (Karen Blixen), *Seven Gothic Tales*

Wine tastings – whether they are small and private affairs
or large and professional ones, it matters not – are worthless, wasteful, wanton and witless. This is why so many
people, both amateurs and wine professionals alike, take
them in such a determined and serious manner. With the
possible exception of gourmet cheese (one of wine's
oldest partners in crime), no other substance is treated in
such a staggeringly surrealistic way. Wine is studied,
sniffed, sipped and quite often spat out. It is discussed in
terms either platitudinously general or moronically jar-
gonistic. Such communication is meaningless, but it does
serve to keep the succubus that is wine lore alive and
well. Wine talk makes art criticism sound positively
understandable. But let's not allow this to put any of us
off attending a wine tasting.

There are three types of wine tasting, and all of them are torturous in their own special way.

The first type is the in-store wine tasting. A wine-maker (very occasionally a winemaker – it's usually the winery's sales and marketing chick) puts up a brand banner in the corner of the shop and pours little glasses of wine for customers unlucky enough to venture into the store at the moment of the tasting. A range of mundanities are swapped between pourer and pouree: the sauvignon blanc is *crisp yet tropical and bursting with pure fruit intensity.* 'Oh, yes, that's very nice. I quite like that.' (It's actually quite sweet with enough residual sugar in the wine to fool the drinker into thinking it's, well, 'very nice'. Sweetness on first account lures you into liking the drink.) *The merlot is our region's speciality and is chocolatey yet spicy with vibrant mulberry characters.* 'Oh, yes; I don't usually like merlot but this one has some lovely flavours.' (Like beetroot and rhubarb. It is a remarkable wine; it tastes under-ripe yet it still has 14.5 per cent alcohol by volume. Those 'lovely flavours' are lying to you: alcohol drives flavour. The wine therefore tastes hot, and obvious.) *We have 10 per cent off all our wines in store today* . . . 'Oh, I can't take too much with me today, but thank you for the tasting. What's the name of your winery again?' *Platypus Ridge Estate.*

The second type of wine tasting is a much bigger affair. It's in the barn-like atrium of a large international hotel and it might feature most of the wines of a particular region, or, indeed, a country. Vinitaly. Vinexpo. Wine Australia. These wine tastings are ostensibly for the trade, although a few mug punters do come along. Mug punters – that's the wine industry's term for their customers, not mine. Strangely enough, few members of the trade bother to go to these wine tastings any more. Either everyone already knows everything or the hotels and convention centres are charging too much money for anyone to run a stall – or get a ticket of entrance. Large-scale wine tastings nowadays only seem to make for wine-industry whingeing. But the fashion industry has its catwalks; and the motorcar industry has its car shows; so why can't wine have a big celebration of its incredible and exciting industry excellence? What was I saying before about selling wine as opposed to buying wine? Once you turn anything into a commodity you are then in the commodity market. Like, duh.

In this sense the wine business is but one or two steps away from Formula One bikini models. Then again, when that starts happening, maybe I'll start going to a few more wine tastings . . .

Or maybe not.

The most torturous wine tasting of them all is the actively organised and RSVP-invited wine master-class. Which is why, should you ever get a chance to go to one, GO. But never go again. One is enough. Treat these events like you would swingers' parties or Amway evenings – which are more or less the same thing. Once – and maybe that's a stretch – is enough.

An embossed invitation came via email attachment, which sort of lost the effect of the embossing. It was (not) handwritten by the chief-head-executive winemaker of

Floodwater Bridge. Floodwater Bridge was a small winery in a posh wine region. They'd made their money before wine and they now lorded it up over anyone who could be lunched to listen. The CEO winemaker banged on about how European their wines were, and how their wines were the future of the wine industry. *'Floodwater has made a small but appropriate start in the highly competitive global fine wine market. I am grateful for the honesty of the Dogbone Vineyard that has produced the goods from quality and "true to terroir" viewpoints . . .'* Whatever that meant.

It was about a 2000-word invitation in which I struggled to find the key information, such as time and place. Eventually I figured that stuff out. It was a Monday, of course; and it was at a poncy fag-hag restaurant in the latest, bestest part of the city. Mondays mean that restaurant managers and sommeliers can come along – because it is their day off. Mondays mean that the winemaker can get the number of seats required. Mondays mean the restaurant will probably do a deal because no one else is going to be in the restaurant actually paying real money for lunch. And Mondays are good because everyone invited is looking for a free way to drink off the weekend's excesses. The only catch is the tasting torture.

Being a posh and aspirational winery, Floodwater Bridge offered us a glass of Pol Roger as we arrived. That might have had something to do with the fact that Daryl Floodwater – the CEO – had seen his daughter marry a Pol Roger executive. But I'm only guessing. I skolled my champagne and asked for another and skolled that too. There's no point selling out unless you are going to get something out of it. The luncheon tasting was soon called into order, however, but not before ranks had formed and the various classes of wine society had been delineated.

At the top of the league table is Uncle Bulgaria. Well, that's his industry nickname. He is one of the world's leading wine experts and writes innumerable articles about the tastings he goes to in Malta, the Hunter, Central Otago, Bolivia, Burgundy, and Et Cetera. He is the wine personified, in its old English sense. Wine is more important than people. The fact that he had been a lawyer before his wine career helps his general presence. Around Uncle Bulgaria hangs the winemaker of Flood-water and a few other key wine-industry Triple-A types. A wine auctioneer, who happens to be an Englishman. A wine scientist, who happens to be German. A wine judge, who is unfortunately Australian but has learned to mimic the bullying and private-school-boarder mentality of the others so well that he is considered an equal. Almost. Oh, and there is the subservient wine sales and marketing chick, who spends her entire lunch flattering the silly old half-drunk wine men. She's invariably got an IQ about ten times bigger than the blokes (and she is usually a little bit taller than most of them) but she just doesn't know how to use it . . .

The Floodwater Bridge externally contracted PR professional comes around to all the tables. He can talk under water and under duress and even under the watch-ful eye of the ever-critical Floodwater CEO. Everyone is his best mate; all the girls *look bewdiful*; all the wines are (sotto voce) *roolly smart*. 'Seriously, these are roolly world class. They are world-class wines. No other wines are as world class as these world-class wines . . .' This particular verbal brand reminder was delivered with every ounce of the PR bloke's mental and physical sincerity. All one ounce of it. 'Maaaaaaate . . . Good to see yooooou. Thanks for coming. Top wines today. World class. Maaaaaate . . .'

His suit was OK, his accent was, well, based on something once authentic, but now so stylised and pronounced that it made his words seem somehow theatrical. And, despite the suit, he looked like a failed rugby player. It takes all kinds, of course. And all kinds of ruthless individuals are prepared to use wine as their stepping stone of over-leapeth ambition. May they all fall off a stone one day and drown in the wine lake below.

On the second-rank table are a collection of scruffy B-list wine media conduits. People like me. We do a kind of musical-chairs performance around the table before sitting down, hoping to avoid sitting next to one or two particularly boring or arrogant or fuckwitted fellow media professionals. I hang off long enough to not get a seat, which is terrific. But that means I have to sit with the wine sales professionals and the two twelve-year-old waitresses from Ristorante Luigi whose sommelier couldn't make it because he was in Tuscany buying a bottle of wine for his wine list. This is not a bad outcome – the table, I mean, not the sommelier buying the single bottle of Chianti. The second little girl seems up for it, and likes drinking Pol Roger. So we get another bottle while the CEO is running through his thirty-seven minute introductory remark. The only person writing anything down is Uncle Bulgaria. All of it.

The thirty-seven minute introductory remark concludes with an extensive tasting of thirteen rieslings from Floodwater going back to 1979. Each wine is poured by a rented sommelier into a Riedel Stem – stems, not glasses. No one uses wine glasses any more; only stems-ware. We all get a specially printed notebook in which to write down our hundreds and hundreds of words of description for each wine. I use my specially printed notebook to write notes to the waitress. Uncle Bulgaria finds the fifty-seven page specially printed notebook too small, so uses an old foolscap-style 200-page notepad to review each wine. The English wine auctioneer has an electric notebook powered by Apple. He types everything into something called his database. He needs a special chair and special table to do this, so as to not contract a workplace injury, thereby setting off his wine-industry-related sciatica. Once we have spent an hour tasting these unremarkably dissimilar wines we then have to talk about them.

The CEO starts things off, joined by the PR bloke.

'Well, ladies and gentlemen, if we can now call the first tasting flight to a close. I'll make a few comments about these wines before we move into the second flight of wines – they being the cabernet-based blends that I made when no one else was making them and that are now considered to be classics before anyone else was making them . . .'

The PR bloke's senses tingle. He grabs the microphone.

'Yes, thanks Daryl. We're all certainly looking forward to moving into that flight; but, look, time is of the essence and we know you are all busy people, so let's get down to the nitty-gritty and discuss the outstanding world-class rieslings we have just had the incredible privilege of tasting. And I don't know about you, Daryl, but I didn't see too many people spitting them out. I certainly *drank* mine . . .'

The room now erupts with a barely audible murmur of laughter. No one actually wants to laugh at the PR bloke's line, but there is a deep-felt need within the room's broader if ever-fading humanity that someone must laugh at some stage merely to keep the tradition of laughter alive. Lest wine-tasting kill it for ever.

The room now goes deathly silent. The CEO makes the initial move.

'There's no doubt that the 1979 is an outstanding wine that really typifies what the philosophy was and is of Floodwater, in respect of our passion for a journey to find wine that is made solely in the vineyard, from the terroir, with a passion for wine that is rooted in the soil of the pleo-bronzo-hedo-cloaca-crustaceo geology of the vineyard's vineyard . . .'

Even Uncle Bulgaria can't stand this sort of wine-olgue, so he wades in.

'Daryl, I can only concur that the '79 is an outstanding wine of its type within the spectrum of those wines from 1979. When you think of the lower-middle-upper Mosel in '78 and what riesling makers went through during that summer, ha, ha, ha . . .'

Everyone now laughs knowingly, in accordance with Uncle Bulgaria's initial laugh. No one knows why.

'The point that I think needs to be made is that these wines really do show an exhibited character of linear intensity underlying a powerful acid-driven structure without which the wines would have clearly not developed so stunningly as the '79 before us so obviously has. You don't have to be a rocket scientist to see that.'

Uncle Bulgaria laughs again. No one else does. He looks rather forlorn, as if he's thinking he got that trendy phrase about rocket scientists somehow wrong. He makes a note on his foolscap page asking his PA to look into the phrase 'rocket scientist', to check that he got it right. 'Rocket scientist – professionally embarrassed – check it twice. ASAP.' He then initials the note to authenticate it. And dates it. Old habits die hard.

An über-sommelier with some real courage and obviously some professional self-improvement in mind makes the next comment.

'Daryl, what strikes me most startlingly about this stunning riesling from '79 is the way the citric terroir-derived nuances have evolved into the cumin seed and raisin-toast bottle-developed secondary and tertiary complexities.'

As he said this he kept swirling his glass – sorry, his stem – around. And he didn't laugh. Which is what I wanted to do.

The punch-drunk editor of a local glossy wine magazine seizes on this expression of clear thinking to drop into the intelligent *converzatione*.

'Yes. Trent, I think you've got a really important point there about the essence of what these wines are in terms of their fundamental connection to the vines they come from, with that statement about viticultural specificity in an ongoing and bio-dynamic vineyard. Daryl, was the vineyard fully, operationally bio-dynamic as far back as '79?'

'Yes, Paul, thanks for that question. No, it was fully bio-dynamic, but only in terms of the way I was bio-dynamicking in '79, which was before bio-dynamics had really started anywhere on this planet. The French have now copied my practices, but, look . . .'

The PR bloke once again slashes in.

'Daryl, Daryl, sorry, if you'll let me just say that Flood-water's bio-dynamics go back to the original stake-holder-traditional-land-custodians, the Yanga Yanga people, who traditionally respected the land before your family ran it as a highly successful cattle farm and now world's-best-practice winery and vineyard. So, Paul, the answer to your question: Floodgate has been bio-dynamic for 40,000 years.'

Everyone wrote that down.

We now had to deal with the red wine, which was a cabernet thing, going back to, yes, 1979. Twelve wines from that and subsequent vintages were poured into tasting stems-ware before each taster, and then we all had to do the sniff, sip, spit, scribe bullshit. There was still hours to go before the designer lunch arrived. André Simon once commented that wine without food is a ghost. That's how these old, dead red wines seemed. In fact, worse. They didn't even have a supernatural under-tone to enliven proceedings.

A little bit of wine had been absorbed by now and a few people at the tasting were starting to whisper among themselves. Wine master-classes are a bit like being in a classroom – there's a wave of whispering that rises and falls at different moments of the class; there are groups of students that bind together; there are some ratbags.

The PR bloke continued his ringmastering.

'Well, ladies and gentlemen, if everyone has finished . . . Let me just say, Daryl, thank you again for putting on these amazing iconic wines. I think I can speak for every-one here when I say that the wines all look amazingly fresh and young, suggesting many years ahead of them yet, which is no doubt why Floodwater Bridge cabernet has just recently been raised to the highest category of classification in *Pontforth's Australian Wine Classification Guide* – and, Aaron, thanks for taking the time to come down here from Sydney to join the master class today.

Yes, Floodwater Bridge cabernet now joins the likes of Grange and Hill of Grace as one of this country's most outstanding wines. World-class wines . . .'

The little waitress sitting next to me had become a bit more serious during the cabernet tasting and was still agonising over her notes on the twelve wines. I reached across and scribbled on her tasting booklet the words, *A lady would never drink these wines, would she?* She scribbled back, *I noticed a certain gentleman DRANK all of his* . . . True. Even though the wines were fairly foul they at least had alcohol in them. And it was getting on to two o'clock. Surely the über-chef would be dishing up any minute now?

We still had some torture to endure, however. The serious A-list wine experts all felt they had to say something about the wines. This is standard practice at such wine tastings: the winemaker wants the experts to praise the wines in a public forum; the experts want to be heard espousing words of wise and penetrating criticism. You might mistakenly think it is like singing for their supper, but it's not. They really do like the sounds of their own voices.

Uncle Bulgaria reckoned the '79 the best bottle he'd had since the one he'd had in '93 at the San Francisco Wine Experience where he was presenting a tasting flight of Australian cabernet blends. He'd given the '93 '79 98+ points, but today he had given this '79 98++ 'because it was so obviously in such smart and complete form . . .' Aaron, the auctioneer from Sydney, commented that 'all the wines showed true to form, which is, of course, one of the reasons I recently lifted Floodwater Bridge up to 'Outstanding' in our classification system, and why, of course, these wines are still performing so brilliantly on the secondary wine auction market . . .'

Tom, the invariably cranky wine journalist (and another English import), commented on what he considered to be the definitive terroir characters of the single Dogbone vineyard, and that he was happy to debate these points with anyone because that's what these tastings are for, and if anyone wanted to debate with him on what he considered to be the true, definitive qualities of these wines then, please, feel free ... The 'supra-pixellated attack-anthocyanins emerging at the three-quarter palate' were the key to all the cabernets. 'Anyone who can taste wine properly can see this is the common thread in the wines . . .' he commented rather loudly, mostly to himself. 'Oh, yes, Tom makes a very valid point about the nature of the Dogbone tannin structure,' pipes in Paul, the glossy-wine-magazine editor, who is not English but always wears a blue blazer. He rambles on a bit about how exciting it is to see wines with such a positive terroir imprint and gets in first, as he always does, with the group thank you. 'But what really strikes me about these wines is their generosity, which they have to get from you, Daryl. On behalf of everyone so lucky to be here today, may I thank you for the tasting and for the wonderful work you are doing for the industry.'

And these people are supposed to be the critics?

The PR bloke leads the loud if a little too brief applause, before signalling to a sommelier to bring in the fresh trays of Pol. Tom tries to start an argument with Paul about the latter's obvious misinterpretation of the former's tannin thesis. The first tray of Pol goes straight to the 99 per cent male A-list table, despite the fact there are several ladies in the room without a full champagne glass in their hand. Praise for Floodwater Bridge continues. The latest vintage produced 715 cases; the wine retails for $179 a bottle, if you can get it. It is considered a crime to drink the wine – except in professional tastings, of course – at anything less than ten years' bottle age.

Yet all of this is but the bullshit factor. In their own secluded playgrounds, wine animals work – and play – in a very different way.

When the tasting glasses are put away and when the jackets come off and when business cards stop being exchanged, the too-thoroughly professional personnel of wine sales become the naughty fawns and fairies that during daylight hours are only ever glimpsed, and certainly not seen. Wine sales? Yes. All wine is salesperson-ship. Whether you make it or grow it or drive it around in a stretch limo, everyone in the wine business is effectively in sales. The dignity is dead. Wine no longer needs to be bought; wine now has to be sold. To everyone. Even to people who shouldn't buy it. And you can taste that evolutionary change in every glass, particularly if you drink – I'm sorry, you consume – Australian wine. The worst wine in the world.

Oh, here we go. Pilgeristic Barry Humphreyisms are creeping in. This author must poo-poo his own nest. Bullshit. Australian wine is as effortless and comforting as a 1970 Glenvill Homes *home*. Never a house; always a home. Something you can boast about rather than live in. Australian wines are like Australian suburbs: vast, bereft, suicidal and mind-numbingly alcoholic. The kids grow up bungaloid and the pet dogs and cats worse. Only the abandoned housewives survive – old and lonely and watching daytime TV in their mortgage-free prison. Australian wines are as roadworthy and as drivable and as stylish as a General Motors Commodore, complete with a plastic handbrake and fourteen soft-drink holders. But you have to have one of these non-cars to drive to the 'local' shop to buy the soft drinks, because the suburb is so sprawling you can't actually walk to the shop. Australian wine is sickly. Lewd, loud, and – at its best – only marginally grotesque. It is not for drinking. It is for selling. One day the world might find this out. Like they one day might with soft drinks. Uh oh. We take the only water left on the Australian continent and turn it into wine that no one actually needs. No wonder the fawns and fairies party so hard. They are coming to the end of their dream.

The party started at about 8 pm. The tasting had finished at six. Like-minded soulless souls got together at the Exeter Hotel to have a few palate cleansers before repairing to my house in Kneebone Street. To celebrate. Or to party. Or to get drunk. And take drugs. And to get seriously unprofessional. With a creative application and discipline that would make W. C. Fields look like a naïve amateur we all got *very* sideways. The next day, one of the attendees had a man arrive to collect my sofa, in order to take it away and have it humanely destroyed. At the same time he delivered a new one. Decent bloke, the sofa-wrecker; but he had been using the sofa the night before as a trampoline. I think we even broke the ceiling fan, probably as a result of it being turned on and probably because it was directly above the sofa. I mean the trampoline. But they are always one of the first pieces of celebratory equipment to pack it in. They just don't make ceiling fans – or sofas – like they used to any more.

The party started sedately enough. Zac arrived with five girls and five bottles of tequila. He apologised. 'I broke the sixth one – the bottle, not the young lady.' He was a round man with a zest for life and an unadmonished streak of harmless yet expensive naughtiness. Which is why he could, at the drop of a hat, muster up five young ladies to accompany him to a non-entity wine party. He had been drinking heavily all day and he had also been judging some sort of wine show; however the exigencies of time meant that the only way he could get to the party was to drive. A young lady – or even five of them – like to be collected in a car, after all.

Two other vehicles arrived with Zac's. One was a taxi and the other one a sky-blue Cobra replica sports car. Out of the cab jumped four pre-ruddied young men – all winemakers or winemakers' assistants or wine something-or-others. Out of the sky-blue sports car lithely skipped a posh winemaker from a posh wine region. He had a bottle of Dom in one hand and a tiny ballerina-like girl in the other. 'Ben, allow me to introduce you to Inca.' The young men from the cab rowdily removed two slabs of beer from the cab's boot. It was one of those moments. I greeted them all at the door and, because it was a wine event, felt as if I had to talk important talk to the posh winemaker and his leading lady. He was very gracious, of course, and offered to put the Dom on ice all by himself. When one of the boys asked him if he'd like a beer he replied, 'No thanks, I'm driving.'

'What about your girlfriend?' said a rowdy young man. She grinned like a white picket fence and skipped into the house.

More guests arrived. Rebecca – in another cab – had brought two cases of cheap sparkling wine from her place of employment – as well as her assistant lady winemaker, whose name to this day I cannot remember, despite what happened later on. Rebecca was a too-clever-for-school PR chick for a big wine company. She also brought a Chinese cleaver with her. She had just discovered the sabre technique and was keen to demonstrate. Joe, from Tasmania, had brought two slabs of a particularly revolting beer called Crown Lager that he'd won in a pub raffle with him. We all put our heads together and decided that the best way to practice chopping the tops off champagne bottles was to begin with beer bottles. 'Same fermentation inside . . .' said Joe. 'Same technique . . .' We believed him. We put all the beer on ice and all the cheap sparkler on ice and then thought it best to have a few refreshments before we started sabreing the tops off any bottles.

Nick then arrived with his new American girlfriend, Anastasia. She was a Vegas sommelier and knew how to party, or so Nick told us all. He was a wine consultant who spent twenty-three-and-a-half hours of every day travelling to every part of the world to inform winemakers about what it was they were doing not-quite-right.

Robert, the local newspaper wine critic, strode in wearing rawhide cowboy boots; Sam and Samantha, the husband and wife vignerons, came up the hallway with a huge wicker basket of vegetables they'd grown organically; and Miss Fluffachilla perfumed her way into the room with a bottle of vodka in a bag of ice. Fluffachilla was her winery's nickname, and, therefore, her working name. It was all getting a bit hot in here.

The only way I could cope was to light the barbecue.

Squid. Or calamari, as it is often known. I'd cleaned it and stuck the edible bits of it in a bowl with lemon and olive oil and chilli. The barbecue got to white hot and I threw it all on. Zac had opened every bottle of riesling he could find and Robert had fallen over backwards while sitting in a steamer chair under the back verandah. Miss Fluffachilla put his elbow in her ice bag and all of a sudden a romance was born. And the light of the day had yet to entirely fade.

Rebecca took over the music arrangement. She stood at the collection of CDs, throwing anything she didn't like over her shoulder onto the sofa (all of these CDs got stomped to smithereens later on). Once she'd found some sort of *boof-boof-boof-doof-doof-doof* non-musical CD she put it on and turned it up. The girls Zac had brought with him now put down their vodkas and started dancing. Robert thought it wise to add some herbal remedy to his sore shoulder and so Miss Fluffachilla rolled him a joint as Zac tapped me on the shoulder and said there was a problem in the bathroom. We went into the bathroom and the problem was a deposit of laundry powder someone had left, in a neat little line, on the top of the washing machine. 'You should take care of that, Ben,' he said to me. So I did. And then the party seemed a little bit too slow.

So we moved all the furniture outside and Rebecca opened all the other red wine she could find in every cupboard or nook or cranny and Joe rang his mate Matt who then arrived with a dinner-setting for 16 and we chopped up a yard of Scotch fillet that I was saving for a family event and we made minute steaks and over-roasted potatoes for how-so-many people were present and then ate.

And it all seemed so completely natural. In fact, it seemed like a very normal celebratory night. It is just that we didn't really know what we were celebrating.

Which is why we had to sabre.

It is a simple-enough affair. In one hand you hold a bottle of sparkling wine – or a bottle of beer. In the other hand you hold a Chinese cleaver – or a French cavalry sabre. You hold the bottle at a sixty-degree angle, pointing away from you, in an outstretched hand. You strike the very-near top of the bottle with the sword – or cleaver. The top of the bottle comes off, along with the cork – or crown seal. You then pour the wine into a young lady's shoe and drink it before proposing marriage to her. At least, that's what Russian cavalry officers did in Paris after the Napoleonic Wars. Being a responsible host I had the first go at it. With military precision I stood to full attention and swung the cleaver through the near-top of the bottle. Right at the point of contact I closed my eyes. What a wimp. When I opened them I was holding two things: a cleaver and a newly fashioned glass ashtray. And I was standing in a pool of freshly emancipated beer.

We all had a go. Rebecca was the cleverest at it – as she was with so many other things. But we soon tired of smashing the tops off bottles with a Chinese cleaver and that's when Zac remembered he had a pack of children's pretend tattoos in his pocket. And that's when Rebecca's friend and I got intimate. Girls like tattoos on their bottoms; and boys like putting them there.

The end of a dream? Or were we still in deep sleep?

We eventually woke up. Rebecca's friend, whose name temporarily escapes me, wanted some fruit for breakfast. The kitchen had once had fruit in it, but all of that had been exterminated a few hours before by Zac, using a vitamiser and a daiquiri recipe. But the backyard had a peach tree in it. And the peach tree had peaches on it. And we still had a few bottles of cheap sparkling white wine.

Bellinis at breakfast got some of the other overnight guests up and running. Well, not actually running, but slowly groaning about. A nice bloke from British Columbia who was over here making wine for some winery or other helped clean a few things up, and opened the fizz so we could make the Bellinis. The peaches were perfect and almost juiced themselves; the only mind-warping part of the exercise was pouring the fizz into the glass, on top of the peach juice. It fizzes up violently and it takes you about fifteen minutes to pour each one, which is not a lot of fun when you are hung over and tired and rather in need of some Bellini. Rebecca had stayed too and she was talking to her lady winemaking friend about the outrages of the evening before and how Monica had told her that she was ready to find a new boyfriend because she was sick and tired of sleeping with her girlfriends' male friends. 'Like she said to me, "After a while, like, you just feel like you're a cheap slut." Like, no shit Sherlock.'

Her lady winemaker friend chimed in with a chirpy 'Well, I might be cheap but I'm not easy', but then sort of realised what she'd said and gulped at her Bellini. Rebecca burst out laughing and asked her how her toy tattoo was going. The lady winemaker friend went a deeper shade of red and looked at Rebecca questioningly. 'What toy tattoo?'

Rebecca whispered something in her friend's ear. Her friend rushed into the bathroom, where there was a large wall mirror. Seconds later the house was home to a long, girly scream. 'Noooooo!'

It was a late Saturday morning in early February just before a big vintage was about to begin. And this was the way the wine industry prepared for it. Forget the tastings; go to the parties instead.

Wine, as we know it in the English-speaking world, exists outside of society. And that is, quite appropriately, the fault of the English. They, not being able to grow or make the stuff, had to find a different role within the burgeoning world of wine commerce in or around about the seventeenth century. Since this time wine has been intellectualised and it has been separated from its natural companions and surrounds – chiefly: food, friends and family. Nowadays, to be clever about wine you need to go to wine tastings to spit it out with other men you don't know or don't like very much. (It's true, they are mostly men – or ladies doing exactly what the men are doing anyway, which makes them lady-men.) Pretentious intellectualism, rating systems, vintage years and surrealistic adjectives employed to compare wine to plants or animals have won the day. Wine as a beverage, running in unison with cultural, social and culinary factors, has been removed from its sensory and sensual, natural environment. Why do so many English, American and Australian wine drinkers seem embarrassed by wine's Dionysian role? Why do they shy away from sensuality and hide behind the pseudo-intellectualism of the wine bore? Is it guilt? Is it fear? Do all wine bores, before going to bed, take their clothes off in the dark, with their eyes firmly closed?

If wine cannot be unashamedly drunk in a manner

and to a degree that makes us feel a little bit tipsy, if we can't enjoy it freely and naturally, then we need to develop etiquettes to civilise the noble liquid savage. Wine must be discussed. To stimulate this endeavour and to lend to it some shade of importance it is therefore wise to have a few wine writers lurking in the newspaper shrubbery. They must be breeding in there, too, because there are more and more of them around these days. But there's more and more wine around, and more and more people are drinking it. I'm not so sure if more and more people are reading about it, though. It is hard to read about wine because so much of the writing concerns wine, which is unfathomably boring when discussed. I can't even bring myself to read my own ramblings about wine, so I'd be a hypocrite to recommend my wine-typing to anyone else. It is a bit like comparing pornography to sex; as far as this person goes I know I'd rather be drinking wine than looking at it.

A lot of the criticism made about wine writing stems from the fact that 99 per cent of it is written by silly old men who are a bit boring. That's true. Even the odd real lady wine writer seems to have to mimic the silly old men's style, as if that's the only way to write about wine. I don't get that for a second. It's an abandonment of the feminine. It is but another example of wine sitting higher up the evolutionary ladder than Man – and Woman. It is also odd that when we talk about wine we use other animals, vegetables and minerals to describe its smells and flavours. Which makes wine bottles' back labels something of a linguistic minefield. There are a lot of wine weasel words out there. Enough is enough.

It is time for wine to be left to speak for itself. Excepting such mandatory label information as vintage, alcohol percentage, volume and grape variety, it is high time winemakers either learn English or stop mangling the words on their wine labels. Weasel words, jargon and misinformation dominate. Some back labels might as well be written by kindergarten inmates. In Swahili. These back labels make about as much sense as a local-council planning permit. Winemakers, not satisfied that the wine in the bottle is going to torture us enough with its overwrought flavour, now want to further derange our minds via the power of the printed word.

The wine industry does not see this as a problem, of course. The weird wine words, so the winemakers imagine, transport wine to a higher zone of cultural sophistication. And in this rarefied atmosphere things start to take on strange shapes and magical sounds. From it a liturgy is born, understood only by the adherents and devotees of this self-absorbed faith. Given that wino-sapiens exist completely outside normal society, this odd argot never seems strange to them, as it is their language, and a language learned by unquestioning rote. Just consider the verbs used.

Wine makes verbs go all elegant and pretentious. A wine doesn't taste of something or other, it *displays* a flavour (usually a botanic one); even in an adjectival form it is *redolent of* some obscure fruit, like the berry of a hawthorn bush, for example. Apparently this description helps. As long as you know what a hawthorn bush is and as long as you've smelt its berries. Speaking of which, wines do not smell of things – they have *lifted aromaticity*. Of course, this redolent display of hawthorn-bush berries complete with its lifted aromaticity is all down to the winemaker's *philosophy*. And *passion*. Wine-makers, therefore, are both St Matthew and Descartes rolled into one. No wonder then that all their wines are *iconic*.

Being iconic they have the right, it follows, TO SHOUT AT YOU. Some wine labels have to have everything IN BIG LETTERS. The entire descriptive paragraph on the south side of the bottle IS IN UPPER CASE, BECAUSE IT HAS TO BE HEARD. NO, NO: DON'T STOP READING ME OR PUT ME DOWN. LISTEN TO ME! LISTEN TO ME!

Just in case this shouting doesn't get your attention, ever-so-subtle repetition is employed. This from a Western Australian red (and no, I am not making this up):

THIS LABEL SHOWCASES THE CLASSIC REGIONAL CHARACTERS OF 100% GREAT SOUTHERN GRAPES. THIS WINE WAS MADE FROM SHIRAZ GROWN IN FRANKLAND RIVER IN THE GREAT SOUTHERN LAND. THE CONTINENTAL CLIMATE AND GRAVELLY LOAM SOILS PRODUCE FRUIT WITH GREAT CONCENTRATION DISPLAYING THE SPICY PEPPERY CHARACTERS TYPICAL OF GREAT SOUTHERN SHIRAZ.

Characters. There's another one. Wines have more characters than a soap opera in its tenth season. A wine, once again, can't merely taste like something, it must have a *character*. It might have a freshly-cut-grass character; it might have a rum 'n' raisin character (that's my favourite one); or it might have a dried-banana-chip-like character. Seriously. I heard a senior wine judge use that one once, and everyone in the room all nodded and jotted it down. No one seemed to be struck by how ridiculous it was to carve that phrase in stone.

Perhaps this has something to do with the mind-numbing arrogance and condescension that emanates from so many back labels. This from a Clare Valley cabernet:

> Situated in the highly recognized region of Clare, the site was planted in 1969 as a dry grown vineyard on the highly renowned 'Terra Rossa' soils.

Just in case you were in any doubt. At least there's some punctuation at work. Sort of. Highlighting the obvious is very popular, as is the extraordinary use of quotation marks. Here's another one from Clare:

> Following more than 18 months maturation in oak barrels, it has been 'worth the wait'.
> Vibrant crimson bursting with fruit and spice with a soft lingering finish. We are sure you will love it as we are 'over the moon' about it.

Yes, I'm 'beside myself'. It is as if Austin Powers' nemesis, Dr Evil, has gone into the 'back label' business.

If an evil genius can go into the back-label game, then I suppose a spoken-word poet can too. These two lines come from a central Victorian red's front label:

> She smiled and said 'spicy'. He replied 'savoury, but fruity too.'
> Wine is the weather of the mouth.

I'm just wondering how you do a meteorological chart of saliva. And would you want to?

At least they dared to use the word 'mouth'. Wine people usually don't have them. They have *palates*. This is the most frequently occurring example of elegant variation employed in the language of wine. Don't use your nose and your mouth to smell and taste the wine; assess its olfactory characters and analyse its varietal definition at front, middle, three-quarter, back, and after-palate. Then compare it to plants or to animals that most people have never tasted or smelt. Orange blossom, bramble, black cherry confit, wild game, guava, violets. At least they're the ones I like using the most. And it's a one-way equation, too: you don't hear people saying 'Pinot!' when they smell a violet. You don't walk past the orange tree in bloom and yell out 'Viognier!'

Yet perhaps I shouldn't be too grumpy about wine words and their appalling misuse. At least they can give you a giggle, which is more than the moronic use of a score out of 100 does – a system, I'm sorry to say, most wine commentators insist on. *Darling, what do you feel like with dinner? The 92 out of 100? Perhaps the 93 out of 100? Or the 94 out of 100? I just can't make up my mind which one to choose? Which number will go better with the warm salad of free-range Wagyu beef?* Of course, these silly and meaningless numbers bring a finality of judgement to wine; and this means you don't have to think about the wine any more. It's a 94-pointer, you've bought it, it is in your cellar, end of story. At least the words found in the world of wine keep you thinking.

Speaking of which, I almost forgot. There are also some very good back labels. My favourite one is from an Italian wine importer. It's a little sticker that simply reads: *Thank you for choosing this bottle; we hope you enjoy it.* What a wonderful sentiment – or, as the wine industry would say, it displays a gratitude-like character, and is redolent of humility. No, you're right; those qualities will never catch on.

More interesting than trying to describe wine, which, after all, is simply fermented grape juice (or so my *Concise Oxford* tells me), is using wine to describe people. It is more fun than playing astrologist.

A Sydney career stick-chick with a fabulous lifestyle is clearly sauvignon blanc. Chardonnay is a mother of two in an entirely stable but tired relationship with her insufferable, long-suffering husband. Shiraz is a motor mechanic that's made it good, running his own business and employing a lot of people and about to buy a second garage, and all the while not realising that the Tax Office is about to descend. Cabernet sauvignon is a fairly pretentious young academic with absolutely no idea about wine, but who loves to keep a cellar and wear suede. Riesling is a man who does not realise he is a homosexual. He is probably a sommelier. Pinot noir is a hairdresser with a wife, twins, and a new lover called Zoë. He is a cyclist and very temperamental. And dresses like Gianni Versace did on Saturdays – casual excellence. Viognier is an alcoholic PR chick who does not see the spiral she is falling into. Pinot gris is a young woman with interests in the environment and vegetarianism and a complete lack of reality – she can't even see that deep down inside she is terrific fun and terribly funny. She is really grigio, not gris, but she feels she has to be gris so people will take her more seriously and so she can do something for the world. Unlike the thirty-something schoolteacher who is only in the job for the superannuation and the school holidays. Merlot. All too merlot.

Of course, one thing all these people have in common is that they drink wine. Thank God for that. Indeed, to borrow from Benjamin Franklin, 'Wine is a constant proof that God loves us and likes to see us happy.'

7

Alcohol-free days
(and how to avoid them)

Alcohol is like love: the first kiss is magic, the second is intimate, the third is routine. After that you just take the girl's clothes off.
– Raymond Chandler, *The Long Goodbye*

It's more about mathematics than mores; it's more about self-mitigation than Dionysian abandonment. Not drinking alcohol has a masochistic charm. It is everyone's holier-than-thou whip-hand. *I cannot be good unless I am punished; punish me by depriving me of the only worthwhile drug on the entire face of the planet . . . No thanks, I'm not drinking tonight . . .*

Not drinking alcohol is hardly the worst thing a human can do, of course. There are crimes more heinous. Like that one involving the chocolate bar. The chocolate bar sits in the fridge door, waiting for the control-freak to get to Friday evening or to come home from their pilates-combat-yoga class at the gym. Then and only then can the chocolate bar be sacrificed. Because it has been earned. If most of us had earned the right to drink the amount we do then the World Bank would be in a much worse state of affairs than it currently is. Credit-card debt would be but the tip of the iceberg.

Denial, self-control and self-restraint do make some people feel better about things, however. Which is why the notion of the AFD has taken off. The AFD. The Alcohol-free Day. It's a post-modern phenomenon, a bit like awareness wristbands or benchtop espresso machines. Everyone's got one, whether they know what it means or how to use it or not. In keeping with the post-modern message, the AFD is taken as a given; it is never questioned, only praised.

Until you do the maths.

The World Health Organization was once clever enough to punch out a safe alcohol usage guideline. Its principal target was wine. Anyone reading this probably knows the formula. For safe drinking it is best if women drink no more than two standard drinks of wine a day and that men drink no more than four. (That this is inherently sexist seems to have been overlooked by most sexists.) Not only should the two parts of the human race observe this quota in order to ensure a happy and healthy. lifestyle, but they should also practise two AFDs a week. This guarantees important recovery time and also breaks you free from any long-term cycle of addiction. Night doesn't become day and liquid lunches do not roll into debauched dinners. Your two AFDs act as a buffer. All straightforward enough. But let's do the maths.

Two standard drinks of wine a day for women and four for men – observing the two AFDs a week – means that the average genderless person would consume three drinks a day, five days a week. Or, to put it in volume terms, three

150 ml units of table wine every day. A pint for men and a half-pint for the ladies. (God, how things have *not* changed . . .) For the genderless average that's 450 mls a day, five days a week. Or two-and-a-quarter litres a week. Or 117 litres a year. That's about eighty-eight bottles, give or take the odd bit of spillage, breakage or corked wine. For men, 156 litres per annum; for women, seven-eight.

Before we go on, it might now be an appropriate time to reveal that three in ten people you pass on any day in the street are teetotal. That's all I want to say about that.

Let's move on. So, 117 litres of wine per capita, on average, as in accordance with safe wine-drinking guide-lines as formulated by the World Health Organization . . .

The French nowadays drink just less than sixty litres per capita. Ditto the Italians – indeed, they are now closer to fifty. The USA's proud and free consumers average about nine litres; Her Majesty's loyal subjects in the UK quaff about seventeen, but that's rising. The Austrians drink twenty-seven, which puts Australians to shame. Australians – people who grow and make and sell so much of the New World's wine – only drink about twenty litres per capita. And that's been stable for about a decade and a half. No one anywhere else in the world comes close to the WHO's recommendations. The Portuguese, back in the early 1970s, got to ninety-two litres, but that's about as close as any human community has ever got to the ideal level of healthful and endorsed wine consump-tion. And that was in Western Europe's only third-world country, run by a crackpot, if well-mannered, despot. Maybe the fact that no one drove anywhere helped them reach this figure?

I often wonder what my own country – Australia – would be like if we were all on 117 litres of wine per capita? I reckon Australia would have better cars, about three more commonly spoken languages, a much more tolerant attitude to immigrants and a much less tolerant attitude to parliamentarians and parking inspectors. We would probably all smoke more, which is something only Australian teenage girls seem to do nowadays, but what was I saying about sexism before? And what about the teetotallers? There are clearly a lot of passengers in those demographic figures. Particularly given the amount of extra and very hard work – often late-night work – that some beverage-industry professionals have to do.

But why do they do it? Is having a drink, as Raymond Chandler put it, just like taking a girl's clothes off? Is this why we surround alcohol's consumption with all the rules and lore and tradition and anecdote? Is all of this connoisseurship or is it just porno-grography? Can AFDs be like a break in the marriage, a trial separation? Can they serve to rekindle some long-lost passion and romance? Or do people just do AFDs for health reasons?

Of course, some people observe an AFD because they feel so terrible as a result of too much drinking the night before. Hangovers send us running away from the bottle – and not to work. We get hangovers because our bodies fail to cope. I mean, irresponsible people get hangovers because they fail to do the training. In the year 2001, in Australia, employers wore to the tune of $473 million the 2.6 million combined sick days their staff indulgently claimed. The National Drug Strategy Household Survey examined 26,744 Australians and on the basis of those interviews confidently concluded that 2,682,865 days were lost to 'alcohol use' in a single year. This was thirty-four times more than estimated in earlier studies. Low-risk and infrequent drinkers accounted for up to 66 per cent of alcohol-related absenteeism. The report suggested that functioning alcoholics were mostly managing to go to work the next day. Or any day, come to think of it. As anyone who drinks can tell you, work is the best place to get over any kind of mild hangover. If you are going to spend the morning and possibly the afternoon feeling hung, then you might as well be at work, failing to be productive, rather than being at home and lending more economic power to alcohol-related absenteeism.

All the science and all the sociology don't put Humpty back together again, however. When you fall off the wagon and hit the ground, that can be it. The trick is knowing how to land. You can smash to pieces or you can fall and roll. Fortunately it was the latter for me – on the day I got drunk for ever.

I was thirty-seven and a quarter. I had a cold and I had just paid my annual tax and I was tired and I was running behind with work. And I woke up at 6 am like I always do but then I lay in bed before realising it was 11 am. I went to the office and had a Bloody Mary and went to the bank to process some cheques and I got really cranky with the teller. I went back to the office and opened a bottle of wine and ate a steak and halfway through I realised I was drunk.

For ever.

I was now more alcohol than I was human. It was time to tip things back into the balance of the human. I'd give up grog for a while. A few months. A few weeks. A few days. But how do you give up alcohol? Therapy? Drugs? Hypnosis? Jail? Or do you just give up?

AA . . . No, I didn't go to the phone book and look up the A listings for anti-alcohol. I didn't ring *Triple-A Alcohol-Off Services – 24 hours a day, 7 days a week*. The thought of giving up alcohol made me instantly think of Alcoholics Anonymous – that mostly mysterious non-organisation wherein small groups of people with alcohol addictions sit around in church halls or other such meeting facilities talking about drinking. Or not drinking. First-name basis only, for purposes of privacy, of course. Nothing to to do with bad memory. But it didn't really sound like my scene. I'm not very social, and I don't much like talking about myself – not even the good things, let alone all the things I am deficient in. But maybe AA could help me?

It helps just under two million people all around the world every year. Starting in 1935 in America, it was the creation of a drunk stockbroker and a drunk surgeon. These two men met at a church service, and through their discussions and new friendship realised they could help one another give up liquor. They did. Hallelujah. But then, like any reformed whateveric, they had to go on to try something bigger and better. It's a replacement addiction, of course. (Just look at Paul of Tarsus.) So next up they devised AA's Twelve-step program.

1. *We admitted we were powerless over alcohol – that our lives had become unmanageable.*
2. *Came to believe that a Power greater than ourselves could restore us to sanity.*

3. *Made a decision to turn our will and our lives over to the care of God as we understood Him.*

4. *Made a searching and fearless moral inventory of ourselves.*

5. *Admitted to God, to ourselves and to another human being the exact nature of our wrongs.*

6. *Were entirely ready to have God remove all these defects of character.*

7. *Humbly asked Him to remove our shortcomings.*

8. *Made a list of all persons we had harmed, and became willing to make amends to them all.*

9. *Made direct amends to such people wherever possible, except when to do so would injure them or others.*

10. *Continued to take personal inventory and when we were wrong promptly admitted it.*

11. *Sought through prayer and meditation to improve our conscious contact with God as we understood Him, praying only for knowledge of His will for us and the power to carry that out.*

12. *Having had a spiritual awakening as the result of these steps, we tried to carry this message to alcoholics and to practise these principles in all our affairs.*

(Newcomers are not asked to accept or follow these Twelve Steps in their entirety if they feel unwilling or unable to do so.)

The first three steps introduce the notion of God in a very slick way. Step 1: your powerlessness. Step 2: a higher power. Step 3: God. It then pretty much becomes a prayer meeting, but it is nice to see that Step 8 inspired a TV sitcom – *My Name is Earl*.

AA claim to be anti-organisation and non-governmental. Indeed, much more than that:

Alcoholics Anonymous is an international fellowship of men and women who have had a drinking problem. It is nonprofessional, self-supporting, nondenominational, multi-racial, apolitical, and available almost everywhere.

There are no age or education requirements. Membership is open to anyone who wants to do something about his or her drinking problem.

Fair enough. But it is religious. Fair enough. But it doesn't say so. It doesn't say it is a religious organisation. It denies this as much as its members once denied they were alcoholics. This might be why some critics of AA reckon it no more than a successful cult. A bit like Christianity, one must suppose.

Critics claim that AA members become dependent on their AA group instead of alcohol. Critics suggest AA has wrangled alcoholism into an addiction corral – America treats alcoholism in exactly that way. An alcoholic is an addict. The only way to beat the addiction is total abstinence. But the message is more severe than that. It hints at that puritanical streak that's always just below the surface of American society (despite the fact that the US imports more alcohol than any other country – and by a country mile). If you've had a few too many drinks on Friday night, hey, maybe you've got a problem. Maybe you should go to AA?

Another subterranean American tendency also comes out. In Robert Altman's 1992 film *The Player*, Tim Robbins' movie-producing character, Griffin Mill, excuses himself from a meeting, saying he has to go to AA. *I didn't know you had a drinking problem*, comments another character. *I don't; it's just that's where all the deals are nowadays being done . . .*

AA's quasi-religious leanings are also mimicked in the very nature of its co-counselling. Like a prayer group, you sit around and talk about how worthless you ultimately are but how that's OK because you're managing to stay off the grog. It's therapy but it is not therapeutic. You don't get better; you simply avoid the problem. Your personal weakness and the profound evil that is alcohol is the crux of your weakness. It's a forgive-me-Lord-I-am-weak-you-are-strong capitulation. AA is a creation, a new world, wherein you can successfully fail to confront your problem with alcohol for ever.

But two million members worldwide cannot be wrong, can they? Besides, AA is sort of like the only alcoholics' survival franchise going around. There's not a lot of competition.

In many European countries, where drink is king, thoughts of AA are as fantastical as thoughts of speeding limits and parking restrictions. American Prohibition gave rise to Alcoholics Anonymous. Both are forms of the same internalised guilt. Both proclaim God and both argue abstinence. And Jesus' first miracle was turning water into wine for a thirsty wedding party. So should I really be going to AA? Should I really be trying to give up drink entirely?

Of course not; I just needed a holiday from it. But maybe an AA visit could work like a tune-up on an old car. Maybe one meeting could knock a bit of shape into my befuddled body and tipsy mind. Besides, I was a bit curious.

The closed meeting was on a Monday night eerily close to my house. Held in an arts and crafts room of a Catholic Church, the fun began at 8 pm.

'I'd like to welcome a couple of new faces tonight, Ben and Natalie . . .'

A man in his fifties, with a black leather vest atop a black T-shirt kicked the thing off. His AA tag was Derek. Or it could have been Eugene – AA is anonymous, after all, and you don't have to use your real name. The arts and crafts room of the church had some very, very bad pottery in it, and some uniquely inartistic drawings of Australian animals depicted in what one could only imagine to be their natural habitats. It was a bit hard to tell. The small room also had a big hot-water urn that boiled up every fifteen minutes or so, and a few old chairs. There was a water dispenser, too, with a cold and a room-temperature tap. I noticed the beverage equipment in every small detail as I hadn't had a drink since the day before.

Derek opened with the Serenity Prayer.

'God grant us the serenity to accept the things we cannot change, the courage to change the things we can, and the wisdom to know the difference.'

This was a prayer that sat at the heart of what AAs was about. Indeed, AA apologists reckon it *is* AA. They might not have a corporate colour or logo, but they have a corporate verbal brand reminder. It is not really AA's, however, because forms of this Serenity Prayer go back through Germany's seventeenth and eighteenth century's Pietist movements, and maybe even back to the meditations of a sixth-century Roman philosopher called Boethius. Be that as it may, and whether the Serenity Prayer is a prayer or a catchphrase, it doesn't matter,

I suppose. It certainly seemed to bring the attention of the attendees together.

Derek continued.

'Having been an alcoholic now for nearly sixteen years, these Monday nights have helped me stay sober for the past, oh, nearly eleven years now. Growing up in the western suburbs my family always seemed to have a drink in their hand – whether it was Mum or Dad, or me Gran, or me brothers. AA has saved me from some of the horrible tragedies that impacted on their lives. AA has also saved me marriage and me job. Driving a furniture removal truck is thirsty work, but now I just have a Coke or a lemonade at the end of the day . . .'

I was quickly starting to think that this was a big mistake. But then a few horror stories began. Truth is stranger than fiction, and doubly horrific.

Heather was a gaunt, shocked-looking woman who might have been in her forties but could have been younger than that; it was hard to tell through her exhausted and heavily remodelled skin and mattress-stuffing hair. She stunk of cigarette smoke. She'd been coming to AA for about five years. Before that, in a career of binge drinking and drug addiction, she'd lost two children. One had been removed from her by the courts following a series of irresponsible parenting decisions. Her three-year-old son had gone to the beach with her and some friends and ended up with such severe sunburn he'd been hospitalised for a number of weeks. He'd suffered partial organ shutdown as a result of massive dehydration. All day his Mum had been drinking. But not water.

Her other son had been taken from her by God. She'd lost control of an old car on a corner of a winding road in the country. It was late on a Friday night and when she woke up on Saturday morning she was in hospital again, this time as a patient. A cosmetic surgeon was asking her questions. Her face was heavily lacerated. Her son was dead. She'd been drinking since Thursday afternoon. She still cannot remember to this day any of the events of the Friday. Her last memory of her son was him hitting another little boy at the friend's house she was drinking in.

Another very fat and seemingly stupid man talked of his levels of debt that he was now getting under control; he talked about his parents re-mortgaging their house to pay off what he spent – or gambled. About half of the people in the room gambled. Which made me feel a little inadequate. I had never gambled because I had never been able to work out how it worked. Like, actually placing a bet was something that I found quite confusing. And here was I thinking that these other people in the room were stupid. This stupid fat man spent what money he had left on drinking, because the gambling made him feel depressed.

A younger bloke, maybe not even thirty, used the name Scott. He didn't seem alcoholic. He looked fit. He looked healthy. He looked, well, even a bit TV. His voice was slow and a little stumbling.

'I had another lapse last week and still feel pretty shattered. It was the one-drink thing again. I didn't go to work the next day, and this is the new job I've just started, so . . . It's made me feel completely crap again, and I don't want alcohol to be able to do that to me any more. I know I have to give it up completely but sometimes it's hard. But alcohol is a disease and that's why I feel like I can talk about it here. I went to see a drug and alcohol counsellor but what we talked about just seemed all a bit airy-fairy. And some of the things he said to me I couldn't understand. He told me that it was a good sign that I didn't drink every day, but I don't really think he got what my problem was – I mean *is* . . .'

A few other people talked. The other new face, Natalie, said a very few words about not being able to remember things and having trouble with relationships. I think she meant one-night stands. Too many of them. No one was under any pressure to say anything. We were invited to leave some change – whatever amount we liked to, to cover the cost of the coffee and tea.

People were looking anxious, anxious to get going. Apparently they had another AA meeting to go to just a few blocks further into the suburbs. They were AA-hoppers. They went from meeting to meeting every night. It was the only thing that kept them out of pubs and off the grog.

I left a two-dollar coin. But I couldn't bring myself to contribute any confessions or testimonials – if 'contribute' is the word I'm looking for. These people drank and had, to varying degrees, shocking lives. Lives mostly past but some still present. All I had was a drinking problem. Or did I? Was I really an alcoholic?

A note in some of the literature distributed at the meeting saw me imagining some frightening futures as I rode my bike home in the cool, dark Monday-night air.

Remember that alcoholism is a progressive disease. Take it seriously, even if you feel you are only in the early stages of the illness. Alcoholism kills people. If you are an alcoholic, and if you continue to drink, in time you will get worse.

I dreamt even scarier dreams than usual that night, but, worse still, I remembered them the next morning. One in particular involved my father being an old and lonely destitute man, with no one to turn to, and no ability to feed or clothe himself; and towards the end of the dream in a sleeping state of overwrought and anguished helplessness I realised it wasn't my father, but that it was me.

The next morning the sun shone brightly. I got to work at about 7 am and typed about the joys of wine till midday. I made a green salad from the salad greens in the office garden; I fried a chopped-up potato in some olive oil and butter and sprinkled the little chips with celery and garlic salt. I barbecued two lamb chops. And I drank more than half a bottle of perfumed and clean Tasmanian pinot noir. I had given up the grog for one full day. It was nice to be home, no matter how close to the wind I was running.

When you give up the drink you get crystal clarity of mind. You remember things. Not just things that happened in the way-distant past, and not just random memory strings. You remember what happened yesterday. Chronologically and in very great detail. You remember what you did the day before yesterday, you remember what you did last week. I daresay if you gave up drink for long enough you could probably remember your whole life, right up until that final moment, when you died from not drinking.

Memory is a tricky thing for keen beverage connoisseurs to, um, remember. There are a few tricks to it, though.

Receipts. Keep all of these. Before you are about to go into any meeting of any kind – with a business colleague, a bank manager, a wife, a girlfriend, both – be sure to have a quick dash through, oh, say, the last three days' worth of dockets. Arrange them in your wallet or purse chronologically, so you can brush up on what you did Tuesday morning before reminding yourself of the restaurant you were in very late on Tuesday night. And who with. This is why it can also be advantageous to annotate receipts. Initials will do, if you happen to know their name. Mobile phone call registers are also handy aides-mémoire. Who and when can quickly lead to why and what – and all you need is the mobile phone's impeccable memory to prompt yours. Using this technique I've often had searingly vivid moments from my immediate past come gushing through the phone's portal into my frontal lobe.

If you are in the sort of work where this sort of vivid recall is an essential part of your job – perhaps you are a diplomat or a PR consultant or a travel writer – don't be afraid to whip a small digital camera out every now and then. Or use the one in your phone. A quick snap of the person, place or event works wonders when quickly replayed the minute before you have to refer to it.

These little professional tips can help you keep on the straight and narrow. Or at least seem to keep you on it. A beverage-induced poor memory is certainly never helped if you are in the often very necessary – if unfortunate – business of having to make things up. White lies. Too many white lies and you can go snow-blind and never see or recognise the truth again. But deceit in any form is a personal, very human condition. It is in no way triggered or exacerbated by alcohol.

Alcohol has not always been considered the great evil, of course. Far from it. Long before we started taking spirits after dinner, for pleasure (or even during dinner, or even before dinner . . .) we took spirits to cure our ailments. Alchemists of the early Renaissance called distilled spirit the *quintessence*. Distilled spirit was, in the minds of the alchemists, the true essence. It was *aqua ardens*. The man responsible for bringing spirits into medicine was the same man who brought medicine into universities. Taddeo Alderotti was a fourteenth-century physician. At Bologna University he chopped up dead things and wrote codes of practice for would-be medical students to observe and, hopefully, apply. Alderotti considered spirits from the ground up, writing about how to distil them and how to use them as powerful curatives. There's no mention of sipping them in a short glass over ice, or mixing them with grapefruit juice to make a lady's cocktail. Spirits were seen as strong and effective medicine, and used as such; and many of Alderotti's recommendations from nearly 700 years ago have only recently been abandoned. Modern pharmaceuticals, with their scarily scientific qualifications, turned spirits out onto the street, and for spirits to survive they've all had to go into the entertainment or hospitality industries. *Keep walking* indeed . . . One wonders how many centuries it will be before Panadol is a sophisticated pharmaceutical of choice, to be taken only when wearing tuxedos and sitting on white leather banquettes. Sounds silly, doesn't it? But go into the past rather than into the future and see what Alderotti was suggesting. Spirits were very effective used as a local disinfectant for any sort of wound. Spirits were a wonderful rinse (but rinse only) to combat toothache. Spirits were mixed with such things as rosemary and sage, then taken as a tincture to cure worms. Spirit mixed with wine and honey made a similar tincture to aid memory. Spirit rubbed into breasts fixed breasts. We are not sure of what, but Alderotti was very keen on this method. Perhaps not all of his practices should have been abandoned? Perhaps not all of them have? Young men still lick tequila from young women's belly buttons. I just didn't realise that it was a medical procedure.

Of course, for real medical emergencies, the most powerful curative of all is one of the most loathed and yet also loved spirits in the world: grappa. It is an Italian white spirit that is used at either end of the day, taken with or in the first espresso of the morning, and then taken with or in the last espresso of the very late night. Of course, it is also taken as a corrective during the course of the day, with any one of the myriad espresso you've got to drink in Italy on a day-by-day basis; and it is also used neat as a digestive or as a health drink at any moment when you feel the phrase 'See you blokes later' coming on. In this way it is one of the most beguiling and dangerous white spirits in the world. And to think that it begins life as little more than leftover – the smashed-up skins and pummelled pips of the annual wine harvest. Nothing more than the leftovers of the wine produced from that year; but what a valuable by-product. These skins and seeds – the pomace – still have enough fermentable get-up-and-go in them, and they are still capable of that one mighty miracle – alcohol. But by-product is maybe too pejorative a term; pomace is better, even if the term does derive from cider making. *Vinacce* is the local term for skins and seeds. Yet maybe none of this matters, particularly given that everyone is crazy about recycling nowadays. In grappa's case, the grapes – just like the carrot peelings that go into the compost bin – are loved not just once, but twice. And the winemaker can make money at both ends of the deal. Grapes make wine and spent grapes make grappa. And the good folk at Carpenè Malvolti in Conegliano, just north of Venice, understand that all too well. No wonder its family owner, Dr Etile Carpenè, could fund the wine academy in the town – one of northern Italy's most important winemaking schools. No wonder he could host the World-Wide Prosecco Trophy, known as *The Golden Flute*; no wonder he could marry into old Venetian royalty; and no wonder he could offer me just about the best Cuban cigar I've ever had, just two seconds into shaking my hand and welcoming me to Conegliano. No wonder I reckoned grappa was all right. Then again, there was a little bit of personal history. Grappa had once saved my life. And at the same time it had protected me from the Swiss. Furthermore it had made me see one of Australia's greatest exports and one of the world's greatest soap operas in a whole new white-spirited light. *Neighbours*. Grappa made me understand *Neighbours*. In Switzerland. On my deathbed. Well, almost.

Winterthur lies twenty or so kilometres north-east of Zurich. I was en route there to visit some distant family friends – a Swiss couple who had once lived in Australia for a year or two on one of those mindless teacher-exchange programs. They taught little kids how to spell and how to make macramé in between driving a Kombi van around Australia during the never-ending school holidays so they could wear no clothes on north Queensland beaches and meet Aboriginals in the Northern Territory. I hadn't seen them for ten years. They lived not far out of Winterthur in a sixteenth-century barn and ran one of Switzerland's most northern vineyards, growing pinot noir on the slopes of Schloss Schwindegg. Walter pruned and picked and made the wine, which he sold to Germans. He had an old tractor in the sixteenth-century shed and a semi-automatic gun behind the door. He also had one of those all-black Swiss bicycles that members of the Swiss reserve army used to have. His wife, or do I mean the woman to whom he was husband, was called Verena. She had three volunteer jobs. One at the kindergarten, one at the old ladies' home, and she was also the local fire chief. Oh, and Walter was also the region's tax collector.

Arriving at their house, seeing them again, taking it all in – it was like I'd arrived at some sort of *Little House on the Prairie*/Legoland/Woody Guthrie/Swatch/Hippie Utopia. But I was fairly sick. I was coughing and sneezing and my limbs were all wobbly and I struggled to lift the luggage out of the back of the car and Verena looked at Walter and said that she thought I might be quite sick and maybe I needed to rest.

It was one of those combined gastro-influenza phantasms that go through you with thorough effect. I lost about three stone over three days. And all of it I spent in the sixteenth-century barn's spare room. It had a big double bed in it and an enormous wardrobe that would've passed for the entire Swiss cuckoo clock section in some Japanese department store. The only other thing in the room, besides the bedside table, was a television at the end of the bed. It had a remote control. My drinking had started thusly, and now I wondered, as sick as I felt, whether it would end this way. The big bed even had a roly-poly beanbag feel to it.

While not being sick enough to feel like dying, the televised programs soon pushed me towards suicide. Only one channel came through. It ran repeat episodes of *Neighbours*. Or, at least, every time I came to, it was showing another instalment. Mesmerised, I felt I had to look; it was akin to being on one of the outer circles of Dante's Hell. I was helpless yet transfixed. But I had one weapon. Grappa.

Coming from Italy I'd bought a bottle of the stuff near Vicenza, from the Brunello family. The Brunello family have been at the grappa game since 1840. Three brothers now run the distillery at Montegalda, halfway between Vicenza and Padua. They are helped at every turn by most of their extended families and a handful of moustachioed men whose every movement of manual labour looked like it was occurring in extra-slow motion. The process is fairly straightforward. Fresh pomace delivered direct from the winery – still very humid and 'alive', as the Brunello boys say – goes into the copper still's heating chamber. The heat comes on and the paranormal power of the distiller comes into practice. Seems easy, doesn't it? And it seems very easy to stuff up, too.

The finished grappa runs one last hurdle before it goes into two years of settling and storage: it has to pass through an Italian government meter. A tax meter. At Brunello it's much like every meter around the country: aircraft-grey in colour, standing about half a metre tall, with a pipe going in the front and a pipe coming out the back. In the centre is a rounded glass dial, or a grappa-odometer, if you like. It looks just like the water meter at the front of your house – if you're still allowed to have water, that is.

The Brunello boys' meter is numbered 659, which seems odd in a way, because Brunello is the oldest working distillery in Italy. There used to be many more stills, however – about (at the end of the nineteenth century) 200,000 of them. Nowadays roughly 130 remain, ninety of which make the commercial grappa seen dominating airport showcases all over Italy.

The Brunello family distil at low temperatures and at low pressure. Like whisky's heads and tails (or foreshots and feints), knowing when to cut is all-important. 'How long do you cook it for?' I asked, and Paolo Brunello replied: 'It is like a chef and an oven. When is it ready? We only know these things because we were trained on this still. It's learned in the family.' Too true – indeed, Italian wine schools did not produce a distiller until 2004. 'We were not born in a hospital; we were all born here. Maybe that's how we know . . .'

Hospital. By the time I'd arrived in Switzerland maybe that's where I should have gone. But if Brunello grappa could somehow guarantee healthy home-births maybe it could get me through my Swiss Plague.

I would lie in bed and sweat. Then I'd dream awful dreams and wake up wondering if this woken reality wasn't part of the dream too. Then I would see the remote control and then I would see the grappa bottle and then I would press the 'ON' button and take the top off the bottle. And I'd take tiny swigs of Brunello Grappa Bianca at 40 per cent alcohol and watch Australia's soap opera *Neighbours* in 100 per cent French. Kylie Minogue was still in the series. She was struggling to come to terms with her job as an apprentice motor mechanic and her love for Jason Donovan. They would either fight or embrace as the de facto parents and non-relatives in the background would suck on tins of Foster's. Most of the acting was done with hands: they were either confrontationally placed on hips or comatosely wrapped around cans of beer. Most of the acting was done with a monobrow and a flannel shirt. And yet most of the acting was rendered all too charming by two simple overlays: the French-language dub and the Italian grappa hallucinations. In and out of influenzic consciousness I saw *Neighbours* and Kylie and grappa and even the Swiss in a whole new light. And on the fourth day I rose, and fled. Winterthur proper had a good gallery and in it was a collection of Dumas sketches. No longer sick and no longer grappa-pickled I looked upon them as if I'd seen human artistry for the very first time. Whenever I use grappa I still have a feeling for all of this experience.

And I still use grappa in such a way whenever I get sick – influenza sick. As soon as I start to feel those weakened and wobbly, depressed symptoms. I introduce the elixir a little earlier in the procedure, however. Usually with coffee. Morning coffee.

One coffee is often not enough; and two brings on the coffee headache. Three fails to cure it. There must be a better way. I'd try tea as an alternative but tea nowadays seems too alternative in itself. All those infusions and relaxants and meditative tea leaves. Besides, I don't own the requisite yoga mat to make it all fall into place.

Yet I found a solution, and its name is grappa. We all know the drill. Grappa – a pure white spirit used by grown-up Italians to enliven their day-to-day experience. Or even to get them going in the morning. You pour a shot of grappa into the morning espresso and – bang, flutter, bang, whoosh – away you go. Just like tipping a bit of petrol straight into the top of the carburettor . . .

This is the way to try it, at least with morning coffee. Oh, and I should warn you, you need a coffee machine to make all of the following possible. Make a tight and crema-heavy espresso and then add a shot of grappa to the coffee. Throw it back and then go and sack a few people.

Or load up the espresso bayonet fixture with coffee grinds. Attach to the machine and pump through half an espresso. Stop the pump, tip a shot of grappa into the espresso, and then pump a few more drops of coffee through the machine into your espresso. This integrates the grappa a little better, and you don't sack people; you hire them.

Or make an espresso and drink it as you normally would; then add a shot of grappa to the empty espresso cup. Swill it around, slug it back, and do whatever you damn well like. Very popular.

Given that so many people use wine as their dietary staple it is a wonder that it has taken so long for someone to write a wine diet book. *The Wine Diet*. That's the name of the book. Not only is it a diet book, but it is a diet book written by a man with the word 'professor' in front of his name. Professor Roger Corder. He must be a professor because he wears professorial jackets and ties and quite sensible lace-up shoes. His half-balding head and his height give him a sort of Picard look. *We will go on a wine diet. Make it so . . .*

Professor Corder's wine diet centres on polyphenols. No, that is not a petroleum by-product. It's a compound found in tannin. Tannin is found in red grape seeds and stalks and skins. And tea. And lots of leaves and fruits from lots of other plants – like chestnuts, for instance. Tannin gives wine its astringency and its mouth-puckering quality; it also helps slow down red wine's ageing process; or prevents you from enjoying the wine more quickly, depending on your wine pathology – do you drink it or do you keep it . . .

But back to weird names. In wine, the polyphenols are often expressed as flavonoids. Flavonoids are subsequently most beneficial (at least to your arteries) when they are called procyanidins. If you drink wine with this gear in it then, no, you will not look like Paris Hilton, but you will live for ever. Dieting under the tutelage of Professor Corder will therefore not target obesity but that other rather annoying modern lifestyle health challenge: immortality. It is a logical evolutionary and social step: once we all look like Paris Hilton the next thing to do to fill in our days is to live for ever. And, obviously enough, we need to do this looking like a size six blonde hotel heiress. If you think I'm bagging Paris too much, please, don't get me wrong. She stands tall in my pantheon of courageous women. Singularly it needs to be remembered that Paris Hilton brought a quiet dignity back to blowjobs. I mean videoed blowjobs.

Let's not wander too far off-task, however. Professor Corder reckons that the reason all those cigarette-smoking, wife-beating, donkey-thrashing Mediterranean peasants live for ever on their lunches of tobacco, goose fat and EU subsidies is because – when they are not sleeping – they are drinking polyphenol-rich wine. It's the French Paradox. It is the French Paradox rewritten as a quasi-science diet book. Professor Corder also reckons that the best examples of the wine that will turn you into a 140-year-old Paris Hilton is the red wine from Madiran, in the south-west of France, near Pau. Tannat is the red grape here, and it is a tannic monster. Traditional wine lore reckons that Madiran reds need about twenty years in a good cellar before enough gritty tannin has dropped out of them to make them, well, drinkable. Drinking a young tannat doesn't quite hurt, but it does make your face and mouth contort into a weird rectum, wherein it takes on the impression of a spastic budgerigar's bum-hole.

But now I am off-task again. What Professor Corder wants us to do is to buy and drink red wine with a high procyanidin count. Wines made by traditional methods, with long maceration periods, are the ones to go for, if you want to become a 140-year-old Paris Hilton aspirant. Besides Madiran (which is pretty much undrinkable, which is why the Americans like it, and why the people in the south-west of France are so suicidally dour – it is not the Mistral at all, it is the red wine . . .), try nebbiolo, sangiovese or cabernet. These are wines that are built for men and defy easy pleasure. But women live longer than men anyway; which is why they can drink pinot noir so effortlessly, as their menfolk chomp through tannic tannats, playing a desperate game of catch-up longevity football.

A wine diet indeed. This book is just another excuse for repressed individuals to do what comes so naturally, under the guise of *health*. I mean 'medical experts'. I mean 'health experts'. Oh, goodness me, there are doctors every-where but never a good barman when you need one.

8

Nil by mouth: Southern disComfort and similar toxins

*The best drink in existence is the Pan-Galactic Gargle
Blaster. The effect of drinking a Pan-Galactic Gargle Blaster
is like having your brains smashed out by a slice of lemon
wrapped around a large gold brick.*
– Douglas Adams, *The Hitchhiker's Guide to the Galaxy*

William Faulkner once commented that civilisation
begins with distillation. Maybe he should have added,
and ends. Pure spirit is a revelation; impure or bastard-
ised spirit is a debaucher. The greater part of the world's
spirit falls into this latter category. And much of that
is very badly made (or, even worse, very cynically made)
wood spirit. Aged in the cask. Whisky, bourbon, rum.
Some examples of these drinks are proud, honest and
invigorating; but the greater majority are cheap by-
products sold in an aggressive manner to satisfy multinational grog conglomerates' bottom lines. Liberal
conservatives call these drinks a *rite de passage*. Nanny
government compassion babblers won't say anything

about them at all, lest they alienate an imagined elec-
torate somewhere in the boondocks, where these drinks
so often do their terrible trade.

Yes, as you may have worked out, I'm not too keen
on rubbish dark spirits marketed more than they are
made. But maybe it's all because of a very nasty early
experience. And maybe because I'm from those boondocks.

It had been a long time between drinks for me and
Southern Comfort. They say that babies can drown in an
inch of water. From bitter – or do I mean caramelised? –
experience, I know young adults certainly can. I was
eighteen and I was a voter and a licensed driver and
thus empowered had earned the right to draw a social-
security payment on a fortnightly basis. This government money meant I could drive 600 kilometres north to
the Murray River, on the Victorian and New South Wales
border in an old Renault 12, to buy beer and Southern
Comfort and fail to watch, let alone participate in, a
canoe race – the Murray Marathon.

The Renault kept breaking down. And always in the
middle of the day when the sun was approaching its
hottest and when there was little pit-crew support,
because the pit crew were not on the highway but down
by the river massaging the bodies and minds of the
Murray Marathoners – the people in the canoes. It's
about a five-day race and in all that time, despite the
fact I was part of the support crew, I don't think I saw
the river more than once. And then it was at night, in the
dark, and I didn't so much see the river as fall into

the river. Face first. For some time. Steve pulled me out. And so he should have.

We'd got the Renault to the camping ground down by the river. We were somewhere between Echuca and Mildura, but I didn't know too much about the geography. All I knew was that a friend of mine was in the marathon and that my girlfriend wanted to be on the support crew and that as a result of that I had to go along. Me and two mates, as Australian syntax goes, were in the Renault. We arrived at about midday on the first day of the five-day canoe race and we checked straight into the camping ground, went straight to one of the canoe-race checkpoints, said hello to the paddlers, and went straight to the pub. A barbecue at the camping ground was set for about 7 pm. Having had a few beers at the pub, a few beers at the camping ground seemed a natural extension of our thoughtful foray into the Australian bush. After all, we'd put in a long half-day encouraging the paddlers, who were all competing in the name of the Red Cross, which made the whole thing distantly and untouchably charitable.

After the barbecue Steve produced a bottle of Southern Comfort. We were pretty well north of where I usually lived so I should have cottoned on to what was about to happen. The paddlers went to bed. The girls went to bed. Which meant three young men had jack-shit to do but drink manfully. Or so we thought. Maybe we were the girls? Whatever, Southern Comfort had its way with us.

And yet as a drink it has such a lively tradition.

Georgia peach. This fruit is one of Georgia's proudest agricultural offerings. Taking such a peach you would mix its juice with a shot of rye whisky. In New Orleans this was the Pimm's of its day. (It's still not a bad drink – a Bellini for hard-boiled detective-novel readers, if you like . . .) Or you could fix yourself a cocktail by the name of Sazerac. Rye whisky, peach bitters, a sugar cube and a dash of something very uplifting called absinthe. Remove the absinthe, replace most of the whisky with neutral grain spirit (to lower production costs), add more sugar and replace fresh peach juice with a peach concentrate and, yep, you've got the entirely inappropriately named Southern Comfort. It was probably a slightly more wholesome drink back in 1874, when it was invented in New Orleans by a bartender call M. W. Heron. He patented the recipe and sealed his bottles with a strange sort of *caveat emptor*: 'None Genuine but Mine. Two per customer. No Gentleman would ask for more.' Southern Comfort indeed. Or is there something all too sly about that name? Is it an old man in a big Cadillac full of peach-flavoured candy? I wouldn't know; I was just a young man in a small car full of Southern Comfort. And the water of the Murray River. Which just goes to show – always read the instructions on the packet . . . Buyer beware.

It was sometime after the barbecue and the Southern Comfort had nearly ended. The distance from the campsite to the river was short enough that even a drunk eighteen-year-old could get there. The river was low. It's mostly low. It rarely flows, and flows less and less nowadays. In fact, I think that it's stopped. It might even be flowing backwards, to go and hide in the mountains for a few years until the drought goes away.

We swigged the Southern Comfort from the bottle, passing it among three eighteen-year-olds with speed and dexterity. Until Steve fell off his camp stool and until

I retreated to the river. I thought if I took a short swim I'd feel invigorated and ready for the fast-approaching new dawn. I think I attempted to dive into the river. From ankle-deep water. I think I landed on my head. I think I threw one arm out in front of my body, in an effort to swim, freestyle. I think I lay there for a while, struggling to lift my head out of the inch of muddy water, struggling to free the other arm that was trapped under my prostrate body. I managed to bend my head up out of the water on three occasions, gasping in muddy and wet air. The third time my head fell back into the river I felt very calm. Strangely calm. That was it; I thought I was gone. The terror of drowning became in a muted, long two or three seconds the restful, peaceful journey to the other side. Then I saw a bright light and heard a voice call my name. It was a torch. It was shining in my face. It was Steve; he pulled me up out of the river, shining a torch in my face. He'd stopped me from drowning.

'What are you fucking doing?' he yelled at me, all panicky. 'Where's my fucking Southern Comfort, you fuckwit?'

He'd saved my life. And I owed it to his search for his bottle of Southern Comfort.

Bogan Nation. A bogan is a westie or a redneck; they are sort of one step up from trailer-trash people; they are suburbanally challenged. A bogan is a person who doesn't read the broadsheet newspaper, instead they look at the colour pictures of footballers' girlfriends in the tabloids;

a bogan is a person surrounded more often than not by polyester and cigarettes; a bogan is that person about a step and a half away from us all, by direct lineage. Sorry, I mean, by a root or two. I know because I am a bogan with a very virulent redneck past nipping away at my heels. Yet as much as I'd grown up in it and as much as I'd nearly drowned in it, I still had one very formalised and objective bogan social practice to endure. A bogan wedding.

Drinking at, let alone attending, a bogan wedding is perhaps one of the world's great challenges, for it requires you drink not only during the wedding, but before it, after it, and then into and beyond the invisible horizon. And the drink is drink so foul that it would not even be gulped under a railway bridge. Bogan weddings are unfunny funny; they are intoxicatingly awful; they are inglorious anointments of the very worst of our dissolved tradition and ceremony. By the way, that last word is always pronounced *sarah-moan-ee* . . . By a celebrant. Pronounced *seller-brant*.

It starts very innocently. Not the proposal of marriage or the couple involved. But the invitation. You can pick them a mile off, though. Given that there are three types of mail – mail, tax-office mail and wedding invitations – the wedding invitation is never hard to pick. The only trick is to never open it. Pop it into the recycling drawer and hope they don't follow up.

My mistake was to open the thing in the first place.

Dear <u>BEN</u>

It is with great honour and joy that Mike and Hazel O'Flaherty cordially invite you to the wedding of their daughter Kylie and future new son-in-law Tyson Van Belk on the 27th of November at:

Celeste Receptions and Paintball Range, 1277 Majestic View Road, Mt Majestic, from 2 pm.

Ceremony prompt at 2.30 pm. Photos at 4 pm. Reception from 6 pm. Pls bring eskies as there are no handy pubs.

Wedding list at ty&ky@ourwedding!.com.net (min. order $50+GST and delivery charges) RSVP to Mrs H. M. O'Flaherty, 17 Wombat Grove, Fleur-le-Sands, NSW 2013

Charming. The invitation is invariably personalised, it should be said, with a handwritten note, along the lines of:

Hi Ben! So sorry to hear about your sister's baby! Hope you can make it to my wedding! Love! Ky! X X X X

It's no wonder I RSVPed immediately, and in the affirmative. A wedding like this was sure to be funnier than a hat full of frogs.

Celeste Receptions is in one of those just-out-of-town semi-non-rural locations complete with wineries and scone shops and scenic turn-offs. The signs on the roadside actually say 'scenic turn-off'. I always laugh and try to explain the joke to anyone else in the car with me, but they quickly tune out. Or turn off. Maybe they think I am a panorama snob?

The stunning grounds of Celeste Receptions feature a pond (currently being refurbished) and a wonderful specimen gingko tree. It is in the car park. To the left of the car park is the evocatively Edwardian former tea-house and now reception centre, and to the right of the car park is the paintball range. Tyson found Celeste Receptions when he came here for his Buck's Day. On a post-paintball-massacre high he booked the reception centre for the wedding without any consultation with Kylie or Hazel. 'It was completely a gutsy move . . .' he said to me, after the event. 'But that's why Haze reckons me and Ky are such soul mates, cos I knew, instinctively, what I had to do with this stunning reception venue centre . . . Book it. I'd come in straight off the paintball range and they were not gunna say no to me. Besides, I had three paint canisters left over, and if they'd said no to our wedding date I was gunna seriously fuck up their reception receival area . . .' Ty was a policeman and worked in the Traffic Operation Squad, so he knew how to damage something with a paintball gun.

There were about 120 people invited to the wedding. All had driven. The car park was a collection of Fords and Holdens. They'd parked themselves with Fords to the left and Holdens to the right. There were a couple of utes. A few four-wheel drives. The rest were four-door passenger vehicles. About two-thirds had mag wheels.

One *pooftah* that Ky went through dental hygienist's school with had arrived in a new Citroën. It stood out like dog's balls on a bald parakeet. At least it was easy for him to find it in the car park later on.

We milled around and had some pre-nuptial drinks. Beer, a range of UDLs, there was some *champoigne*, and plenty of cola. You'd get your drinks from the O'Flaherty family collection of vintage eskies and make your way back to your peer group and then a bloke called Tripod would reach into his tuxedo's inner jacket pocket and produce half a bottle of Bundy. Bundaberg Rum. The worst rum in the world. *Tripe*, as his mates called him, topped up your cola-filled plastic wine glass with Bundy and then you all talked about how *noice* the vintage LTD bridal cars looked, and how the *broidesmoids* hadn't scrubbed up that bad either.

'Jeez, that blonde one was hot as . . .'

'Tell you what, out of ten, I'd give her one!'

'Trev! Don't!'

'Sorry love . . .'

Thus fuelled, the guests would make their way into the ceremony-pledging area. Here Ky and Ty would arrive and stand and swap vows and possibly recite poetry and talk of the importance of the vows of marriage before friends and family all standing as witness.

None of this can happen, of course, without a celebrant. She was a tall woman and looked about as feminine as that New Zealand Prime Minister, Helen Clark. Her voice was a little deeper than Clark's, however.

'Friends, loved ones, family members, special guests, *loidies* and *gennellmen*, thank you. Thank you for attending this very special occasion. An occasion what in which we join together in this special time and magical place to celebrate the coming together of two young persons so very much in love – Ky and Ty.

'Marriage is so often a celebration of what is the best about giving and receiving. It is an act that personifies the way two people feel about themselves, each other, their family, and their ongoing place within their society. Marriage is a solemn affair.

'Ky and Ty have chosen marriage as their path together as they move together into the future and grow together. Marriage is their way of saying "I love you" and their way of saying "We love you" and everyone saying "We know". And they have chosen this Sioux Indian poem of love to communicate to all of their friends, their family, and themselves, the essence of this feeling. I call on Gabby Chong to read the poem. Gabby?'

A diminutive girl with long, dark hair and too-tall stilettos makes her way to the ceremony-pledging area. She's half Gabby and half Chong and, but for the pierced lower lip, quite attractive.

Crow flies at night.
Black feather call.
Bear talks to all.
Wind speaks to us in words we cannot know.
When seasons end and we see ourselves grow old, we know that love is as timeless as the grass and as long as the snow.

She splutters out the last few words, tears of performance anxiety and joy emerging as she does so. A woman in the front row of the gathered, witnessing crowd drops her camera as she weeps too. Tripe wolf-whistles and skolls his Bundy. Everyone applauds.

Vows are swapped.

'Ty, do you take Ky to be your *woife*; to love and to cherish; to provide ongoing support for; to respect and to listen to; to be in love with and to be loved by; Ty, do you take Ky to be your woife, for as long as you both shall live, Ty?'

Ty stands nervously, as if thinking, or trying really hard to remember something really important. The celebrant whispers to him, 'I do.'

'I do,' he gulps.

'Ky, do you take this man, this Ty, to be your husband, to love and to hold and to fall into his arms and to be completely understood by at all times with full and uncompromised love, to be your ongoing husband, for ever?'

There's another pause; but Ky hasn't forgotten anything, or had any doubts; she's savouring the moment.

'I . . . do . . .'

'*Loidies* and *gennellmen*, according to the Laws of the State of Victoria and as you *alls* stand here before me, may I pronounce Ky and Ty to be husband and *woife* . . .'

The ceremony pledging area is then almost irradiated out of existence by 120 digital camera flashes. Old men and all the women move in for the kill – to thank the happy couple. The younger blokes all head back to the eskies. It is now beer-drinking time, because we've got an hour or two to go while professional videos and photographs are staged.

By the time we make it into the reception receival area most guests are half-cut. One stiletto heel has already broken under Gabby Chong's left fetlock. She's taken both shoes off now but is still a bit wobbly, thanks to the effects of the ouzo and Coke she's been sipping ever so *loidy-loike* from a UDL can – in a stubby holder. Tripe's wife Bree brushed too vigorously against the door frame of the ladies' toilets and scraped half the fake tan off her right upper arm, which draws even more attention to her rather surrealistic Celtic tattoo. It is a dragon carrying a whisky bottle and wearing tartan and eating its own tail. Apparently – in Celtic tradition – it represents everlasting peace.

In the reception receival area there's a big floor plan of the hack-renovated Edwardian teahouse. What had once been four large tearooms was now one big reception venue. The tables were those big round ones that you often see skilfully de- and re-commissioned in large yum cha restaurants by small Chinese waiters. Unfortunately there were no Chinese waiters here, just little girls still in high school and a few older hospitality-industry professionals wearing bad poly-cotton black suits, complete with lapel name badges. 'Rick' was running our section. He came across as only slightly less gay than his eyes were bloodshot. He welcomed us to table nineteen. 'Good afternoon, everyone. Welcome to Celeste Receptions. My name's Rick. I'm looking after your table this evening, so if you have any problems please just let me know straight away! Enjoy!'

His early flagging of potential 'problems' made me figure that that's what we were all going to get, all night. Problems.

So far I'd had a quarter of a glass of *champoigne*, half a glass of *whoite woine*, and about five cans of VB – Victoria Bitter. Despite Tripe's continuing and generous offers I'd not succumbed to any Bundy in any Coca-Cola. Yet. He offered again. 'I'm not really feeling up for any Bundy, thanks, Tripe.' He gave me a knowing look. 'Yeah . . . You're waiting for the good stuff, aren't ya!' I shuddered at what that might have meant. Bundaberg also make an over-proof 'special' rum. Bundaberg Rum connoisseurs (if that is the right word) cherish the stuff, and save it for 'special' occasions. Like weddings, or golf victories, or birthdays called 'the big four-oh'. Bundy over-proof is even worse than their normal muck. But declining an offer of the over-proof gear from a bogan is like saying no to a potentially very violent African native when he puts a slice of raw rhinoceros testicle on your plate. Rejecting such a treasured offering is the height of ill-manners; and it is the most severe form of insult.

'You're waiting for the JD, aren't ya?' said Tripe.

I laughed a little nervously. Just laughed. Best not to say anything, lest I really do offend him. JD. Jack Daniel's. The Old Number 7. Tennessee Sour Mash Whiskey. Bogans use dark spirits like hairdressers use wine. They know every variety and every variety has a time and place. Sauvignon blanc with spicy Asian; chardonnay with seafood and friends; pinot noir with duck; a medium-bodied, cool-climate shiraz with a nice piece of beef. Lean beef. It's very similar with bogan whisky and rum appreciation. Bundy with Coke; JD with ice and mates, *after you've had ya tea*; Jim Beam and Cola pre-mixed cans in the garage *when ya drop the oil outta the mota and bang a new filda on*; Wild Turkey with power boats or twenty-*foist* birthday *pardies*; Johnnie Walker Red Label with a Hugh Jackman DVD ('. . . coz me and Bree can watch his films, like, *together* . . .'); Johnnie Walker Black Label with Christmas Day. All day.

Jack Daniel's Tennessee is completely different from Jim Beam bourbon, by the way, particularly if you are a bogan. Indeed, to an aged-in-the-wood drinking bogan, they are poles apart. They might taste the same and look the same and do the same things to you, but they are completely different whiskies. Tennessee whisky is filtered through ten feet of charcoal. At Jack Daniel's distillery, for instance, they burn mountains of sugar maple down to charcoal, and crush it up before putting it in huge filtering vats. The spirit then passes very slowly through the charcoal before passing through a thick woollen mat at the bottom of the vat. It can take a week or so to filter through this system. But a week filtering through charcoal is equivalent to a year of barrel maturation, even if the distiller uses 'alligator barrels' – the ones with the highest char on the inside. Aficionados reckon the charcoal-filtering method makes for spicier whisky, with less alcohol burn. Bourbon, on the other hand, has more flavour – or toxins. I reckon it is just a matter of very slight variation; it's about minor degrees of foulness, that's all. Both bourbon and Tennessee can do terrible things to you. Whisky tempers can be scary things. It certainly could bring out the worst in the man behind the best-known Tennessee brand. Jack Daniel himself drank three glasses of his own whisky every night. In his older age he'd put a spoonful of sugar into each one, which is sort of what the bogans do nowadays when they add Coke. Old Jack's temper was the death of him, too. He got so cranky trying to open the distillery safe that he kicked it. He kicked it so bad that he got gangrene in his toe. Then all the toes. He wouldn't let any doctors chop anything off, though, and it took him six years to die. He died, quite literally, by inches.

I relayed this story to Tripe as I was drinking some more awful white wine and he was on about his one-millionth Bundy and Coke. 'Shit,' he said. 'Better stop kickin' the fuckin' mower after I've had a few, then . . .'

And then the first course arrived, so it was time to put away talk of gangrene and appreciate the cuisine before us.

It was hard to tell what it was at first. And it came on one of those oddly-shaped, oblongish white plates, or platters, with awkwardly raised rims from which your cutlery would either fall off and onto the table and floor, or off and into the plate's gluggy vinaigrette or sauce. The entire first course was therefore accompanied to the strains of some boy-band's Motown rip-off CD and dropping cutlery. A lot of bogans have trouble with cutlery as it is, so this plate design seemed particularly cruel. I looked at Rick at one stage as he swanked by, and I was sure I could see a glimmer of some sort of satisfaction in his bloodshot eye.

But he could've been laughing on the inside about any number of atrocities currently occurring in the reception centre. The plates, the prawn-mousse-filled filo-pastry delights on the plates, the just-stale-enough verdelho that was the white wine of choice, the promise of the beef or chicken main course and its accompanying cabernet that proved to have as much vanilla and char flavour in it as the Jack Daniel's Old Number 7.

But then came the speeches, and the speeches sent me directly to the JD.

Why are all wedding speeches like twenty-first speeches? And why do twenty-first speeches never mention the duties and social responsibilities and obligations that, for the twenty-one-year-old in presumed attendance, lie ahead? Why do wedding speeches never include any reference to the important moral and social building-block that is the institution of marriage? Why are wedding speeches always a race between best men and fathers-in-law to see who can ineloquently dump as much raucous and immodest and mostly unearned praise on the two runners in the Happy Couple Stakes? Why do wedding speeches never mention the couple, but only the two individuals? Did wedding couples become selfishly 'me-me-me' before marriage did, or did that happen the other way around?

'I suppose some people here might think it a funny way for two young people to meet,' said Ky's dad, Mike.

He had waded into his wedding speech with all the assured immovability of an old carpet stain. He wasn't going anywhere. We weren't going anywhere. The speech wasn't going anywhere.

'I admit, meeting your future husband at a booze bus, while undergoing a random breath test, might not strike a lot of people as a good sign for romance. But Ky saw something in the man holding the breathalyser that night, and he must of seen something in her, *because he let her off!* Only joking, actually. She was a good point or two under the limit. And that's because Ky has always had a great sense of her commitment to society, and what it means to be an active member of it, not just some sort of person going along for the easy ride, if you know what I mean. This is part of the reason she has so dedicated herself to her career as a dental hygienist, and why she is so professional when it comes to her career. The day Ky graduated from her dental hygienist's degree *was the proudest day of my life . . .'*

The old boy nearly lost it at this juncture. He was temporarily overcome with real emotion. It gave me a chance to nudge Tripe while holding up a plastic wine glass half full of Coke. Actually, a quarter full ... I was hoping Tripe would go long on the JD, and he did. Good men in a crisis, these bogans.

Ky's dad went on and on for about four JDs and Coke. We then got to Ty's best man, Kane. Kane wasn't in the police force; he ran a concrete-cutting business, and was doing pretty well. Bogans always live in outer-outer suburbs where roads are constantly being modified and the essential services that run below them – cable TV, speed cameras, et cetera – need to be accessed by trained professionals. Ky and Kane had been mates at school.

He made the usual sounds about how *bewdiful* the *broidesmoids* looked and thanked Mrs O'Flaherty for having such a stunning *door-dah* in Ky and said how stunning Ky looked and made that point twice, which made me wonder just a bit, and then he loosed off a few heart-felt comments about the measure of the man that was Ty.

'I remember we went on this camping trip once, like, when we were still at school. Ty was really into bush-walking and had saved up his lawn-mowing money to buy himself this really completely state-of-the-art back-pack. And it had all these straps and adjustable bits on it so you could, like, walk to the moon and back and not have a sore foot or shoulder or anything else. But it was a bit unfortunate because whenever he put it on and walked, like, he walked like he had a carrot shoved up his arse!'

The room became a flailing sea of beside-themselves bogans, all *laughing like fuck*. Laughing until they pissed themselves. *I laughed that much I thought I was gunna piss meself!*

I downed another JD and Coke and started to re-image

Gabby Chong, who was sitting on our table, opposite me.

Kane now went in for some stiff-upper-lip praise for Ty, and his role as a *plees offasah*.

'Ty might come across as a really easy-going fella, and he is; and he might seem, like, fairly driven about his key areas of passion, like snorkelling; but I know that it's Ty's, like, really amazing devotion to his duty as being a *plees offasah* that is what really makes him the person he is. I know that when Ty is on duty . . . I know that we're all . . . somehow safer . . .'

Now it was Kane's turn to lose it, but the assembled guests saved him with a rousing wave of applause and that's when the bloke sitting next to Gabby made a dash for the toilet and I made a dash for his seat. We had one more speech left – a duet speech by Ky and Ty – and then four members from the Police Band were going to totally rip it up with some Motown classics, dressed in full uniform, of course.

I moved on to a few ouzo and Coke UDLs, and after the wedding waltz and the cake-cutting a few of us ended up back at Tripe's place, where Gabby proved to be very clever at smoking marijuana, and as she and the other girls had a few exotic cigarettes in the lounge room me and Tripe and a few of the other good ol' boys had a few Johnnie Walker Black Labels out on the back veran- dah because *it was, like, a fuckin' special and fuckin' fantas- tic day.*

As Ky and Ty jetted off to Noosa we played Stevie Ray Vaughan CDs until 4 am. And it was a fan-fuckin'-tastic day. Hats full of frogs don't even come close.

Duncan McDuncan is the thirteenth Master Distiller for 1000 Sporrans Scotch Whisky. Founded in 1742, this distillery has been burnt down more times than any other Scottish distillery. It sits on the shores of Loch Omond and it has its own unique breed of cat. A Distillery Cat. This cat can smell smoke, and on doing so will meow. Mr McDuncan not only distils and breeds cats, but he also acts as the distillery's Global Brand Ambassador, touring the world and *telling of the secrets of the Sporran*. His Scottish accent is so pronounced that I wondered if it were real or not . . .

McDuncan has an interesting take on whisky, and on congeners. 'Porridge. That what it be. Porridge that were then beer. Beer then becomes whisky through the prooooocess of distilaaaaation!'

You see what I mean about his weird accent. It's a bit too *Two Ronnies*.

We're in a posh Chinese restaurant in a posh city along with a few other beverage-industry media types. All are here to be run through a Cantonese degustation banquet matched stunningly with a range of exciting new 1000 Sporran brand extensions. Besides the standard 1000 Sporrans Scotch Whisky – 'a thooooosand blends of a thooooosand blends' – there's the Black Sporran, which is vintage-year single malt, a Spray Sporran, which is a twist-top mini bottle of standard Sporran with some soda and lime in it, and a Well Hung Sporran. This is a can of standard Sporran whisky mixed with stout. It has a widget in the bottom of the can to guarantee a creamy, foaming texture.

McDuncan is visiting the Asia-Pacific region's markets before he repairs to India to compete in the annual Elephant Polo Cup. 1000 Sporrans has been a keen supporter of the Cup since its inception in 1927, when an earlier Duncan McDuncan had spent some time on the subcontinent investigating sonti production – India's version of a rice-fermented wine. 'We, that is, my family, wanted to see if there were ways to turn oats into wine,' says the current McDuncan, with a steely if blurred look in his eye. 'If the Indians could do it with rice . . .'

McDuncans have since that time been passionate advocates of Elephant Polo, which is a much more difficult equestrian art than normal polo, 'or even whhhhater polo', as Duncan McDuncan asserts. Not that it is really an equestrian art in the first place. I just don't know what the elephant equivalent of equestrian is. Nor did anyone else at the degustation whisky marathon, for that matter. But we had already had a few refreshers, and, judging by proceedings, would need a few more to get through to dessert.

McDuncan is asked if there's a possible downside to extending the hitherto very simple and old-fashioned 1000 Sporrans brand. Having been recently taken over by a global beverage conglomerate, was this idea a distillery initiative, or something that has been forced upon the McDuncans?

'Noooooo,' blurts the McDuncan. 'A brand is a brand is a brand,' he says, as if that's the end of the answer. We all sit there, a little bit blank, not knowing whether to drink more whisky or handle more chopsticks.

'Ach, let me put it to you this way,' he continues begrudgingly. 'In 1742 my ancestor Duncan McDuncan built a wee distillery on the banks of a wee loch in a wee part of Scotland. Not the Highlands. No, no, no. Not the Lowlands. No. Not Speyside and not the Western Isles. No, no. But in Lossiemouth, in the Grampians. There

were nooooo lochs. We built one. Then we built the distillery. Then we burnt it doooown, lest it fall into the
hands of the English. We burnt it doooown on multiple
occasions. And so was born the spirit that is the fire
and the heart of 1000 Sporrans. From the carnal flame
comes the spirit that is the beating drum that be the 1000
Sporrans!'

He said this triumphantly, a bit like he said everything
triumphantly. I wasn't too sure whether we had an answer
or not. But this sort of theatrical and ridiculous brand
spruiking was nowadays very typical of the two or three
big multinational liquor businesses that ran all the liquor.
They had to splash a bit of cash around and send heritage-
indicators – like McDuncan – to far-flung parts of the
world in order to lend the current cycle of indistinguish-
able brands some sort of authenticity. Just a glimmer of it.
Just a veneer. A bare veneer. A veneer of authenticity so
manufactured and weak that it could be peeled off and
reapplied to the next invented version of a cyclical drinks
phenomenon. And a new way to sell alcohol.

Substitute a hydroxyl radical for an atom of hydrogen
in a hydrocarbon and, hey presto, you've got alcohol. Get
enough of it together, and get it to at least 95 per cent
pure, and alcohol will ignite at 11°C. Most of us just drink
the stuff, however. Nevertheless, there are some alcoholic beverages that should be burnt. Or used as a broad-
leaf weed herbicide. To clean drains and possibly remove
rust from car-parts. Possibly even to fuel light aircraft.
But they should never be drunk.

These are the top ten worst drinks in the world.

Kahlúa, Tia Maria, Baileys Irish Cream, Cynar, Galliano, Malibu, Midori, Southern disComfort, and retsina. And 99 per cent of home-brewed beer. All are sickly, most are sweet (even the home brew), and none lend any improvement to mankind in any way whatsoever.

Kahlúa is around about 25 per cent alcohol and is the second-biggest-selling liqueur in the known universe. It is the basis of 387 cocktail recipes and counting. And it is as saccharin as hell. Tia Maria is another coffee liqueur and is made by the same mob that make Kahlúa – Pernod Ricard, the drinks giant. In fact, I think Pernod Ricard make everything now. Tia Maria when compared to Kahlúa is the same, but different, as the Australian TV characters Kath and Kim would say. (They also suggest the ideal food match for Tia Maria: Footy Franks.)

Baileys Irish Cream is made by the Bailey family and it is Irish and it does have cream in it. And whisky and coffee and chocolate flavourings. If you mix this liqueur with Tia Maria and Kahlúa the earth then stops and we all get off. Cynar is a liqueur made from artichokes. This is equivalent to artichoke genocide. Galliano was invented in 1896 by a distiller called Arturo Vaccari. It is golden yellow in colour, and Vaccari made it this way because he planned to sell it to the thousands of Italians departing for the American gold rushes – as a crappy reminder of their homeland and as a reminder of the golden future to be found in California. It's been a very cynical drink right from the start.

Malibu always makes me laugh because I think of Lisa Simpson's doll, Malibu Stacy. If only the drink were that funny. It's 40 per cent rum and coconut made in Barbados. Where it should stay. Midori is the Japanese word for green and it is another liqueur-cum-cordial mostly taken by young persons. It's melon-flavoured and about 20 per cent alcohol and made in Mexico. So there is really nothing natural, let alone logical, about it. Southern Comfort is 40 per cent alcohol and was the constant companion of Janis Joplin. The only clever thing she ever did with a bottle of it was bash Jim Morrison over the head after he pulled her hair. Maybe she should have swung harder, then we could have been spared that 'American Prayer' spoken-word rubbish he produced.

And retsina. What can one say about retsina? Of all the ancient practices that should have survived from the early Classical Greek era, why did we hang on to retsina? Three thousand years ago they lined amphorae with the resin of the Aleppo pine tree. This resin acted as a barrier to air spoilage; it kept the wine therein stored fresher, longer; it also gave it a pine resin flavour, which in time people became not only used to but also loved. It is the ancients' version of bad bourbon, I guess. Bourbon is, of course, a drink often consumed by young men who like to home brew. In a food-grade plastic beer fermenter you tip a can of malt extract and some dried hops, a kilo or so of refined sugar, and top the whole thing up with warm water. Pitch the yeast in the top, screw on the lid and fit the airlock, so that gases from fermentation might escape and not cause the fermenter to explode – like the subsequently filled bottles can if the beer hasn't properly fermented. Which it rarely does, because kitchens aren't breweries and bourbon-drinking mechanics aren't brewers. And the extra sugar, or dextrose, always leaves a particularly syrupy aftertaste in your mouth. Home brew just doesn't refresh – part of the reason also being the fact that it is ale. Top-fermented ale, not bottom-fermented lager. But, that said, about 1 per cent of all home brew is, well, not terrific, but pretty good. One tip: don't add any extra sugar; just rely on the malt extract to ferment the beer out to about 2.5 per cent alcohol by volume. If you want a drink to get you pissed more quickly, head back to the bourbon bottle.

There's a reason the bad dark spirits get you wobbly and badly wobbly, too. Congeners.

The toxins that cause hangovers are hard to pin down. They may come from alcohol or they may come from the process your very own body undertakes when breaking alcohol down in order to metabolise it. Alcohol is a drug, but to a lesser degree a toxin. But that's a bit like saying uranium is an entirely safe and natural product.

Anyway, we all know that during the detox process of alcohol metabolism we use a lot of water. Dehydrating affects bits of our bodies, like the brain. This is why we get the headache when we get the hangover. Our brain is shrinking. But of the three evil ingredients in alcohol, one stands out and always guarantees a shocking after-effect. Ethanol might be alcohol and that might always be the fall guy; and acetaldehyde might be the by-product our bodies produce to metabolise alcohol, which, in turn, makes us feel a bit sick; but there's one element in some drinks that is a killer: congeners.

Congeners are impurities born from fermentation and more general alcohol maturation processes. They are a bit of a Janus. On one hand, they add to the flavour, smell and colour of many of the spirits and wines and liqueurs they work for; but they also contribute quite powerfully to hangovers. Ethanol might set the hangover up, and dehydration might put it in motion, but congeners knock it into outer space. Dark spirits aged in wood have a lot more congeners than clear spirits or white wine. Inexpensive dark spirits have even more congeners because of the cheap and quick way they are distilled. Or quasi-distilled. Figuring a congener count, I reckon good vodka is at about one, on a scale of one to ten, and that bourbon – even good bourbon – is at ten. This puts single malt at six, rum at eight, and gin at two. Tequila is not on the scale because it cannot count. Nor can the people who regularly use it. Red wine is about .75. Unless it is from South Australia and being drunk by a lady, and then it is close to four. There you go. The Canaider Congener Scale. If I don't get a Nobel gong for that then the world really has gone silly.

Rum and its history are entwined with enslavement and depredation. Which makes it a strangely suitable drink to abuse yourself with on a Friday night in a shopping mall. But rum, we must remember, was only made possible in the first instance by a handy supply of sugar-cane by-product. Which is why it set itself up in Australia, which to this day makes some of the worst rum in the world.

Bundaberg Rum. Its label mascot is a polar bear.

One thing about Bundaberg Rum, as I've said, is its unique suitability to drinking while undertaking a shopping-mall cruise. You'll need a buddy (as rum drinkers say), and you'll need an outer-suburban shopping mall. And you'll need a Friday night, and to make it really memorable you'll need your girlfriends there, with an arrangement to meet them later on, before the film starts, and after they've done their clothes shopping. You might only have about three hours, but it is amazing what you can do to yourself – and how many liquor outlets you can so surprisingly find – in a sprawling Friday-night shopping mall.

We started in the food court, where we left the girls. We'd all initially met in the food court, because that's where Tan wanted to meet, and she was the alpha male of our group of four, or our group of two couples. Her bloke, Greg, was a computer salesman in-between jobs. It was summer and he was sort of holidaying and playing a bit of cricket on the weekends. So Friday night made perfect sense. With luck, his side would bat the next day and he could spend most of the morning in the pavilion wearing off his hangover.

Once the girls had stopped talking and had decided to head off to buy 57 fabulous and essential wardrobe items, Greg and I were left to our own devices. Sort of. Tan figured that there was little chance we could get into any serious trouble in a sprawling shopping mall. 'All the girls in this place are either schoolchildren or ugly shop assistants, so there's no chance of you striking it lucky, Greg.' Tan and my inamorata high-heeled away. When they were out of visual distance we asked the Sri Lankan guy who came to clear our coffee-booth table if the Italian Coffee Ristorante had anything to drink.

'You mean, you would like a new coffee?' he asked.

'No, we were sort of thinking of a something a little stronger,' we replied.

'Oh, certainly. If you look in the very last page of the menu. Thank you.'

No, no. Thank *you*. For a shopping-mall Italian Coffee Ristorante you could certainly drink. Glasses of house

champagne, white and red – all from one range of south-
east Australian big-wine-company wine. Yuk. You could
get three types of beer: Foster's, VB, or some sort of light
beer muck. They'd certainly all be warm. But you could
also get Bundaberg Rum. You could get 30 millilitres of it
for $6. For an extra dollar you could get it with Coke or
milk. Or both. I kid you not.

We ordered two and sank them before the Sri Lankan
bloke had walked away from the table. We then ordered
another two immediately. He brought them back about
ten minutes later and gave us a wary look when he put
them down on the table. They didn't look like the full
30 millilitres, either. And when you are buying drinks in
volumes of 30 millilitres you need all the millilitres you
can get, let me tell you. Not having had enough alcohol to
feel too over-confident we sipped our final two rums and
paid the bill and quietly headed off. We did a circuit of the
food court, but the Italian Coffee Ristorante seemed to be
the only place serving the hard stuff. Everything else was
sushi or noodles or fried chicken or juice or slices of
pizza with bottles of mineral water.

That's when Greg remembered a football store
upstairs with a 'sportsmen's bar' attached. 'It's got a big
TV with footy on it all the time, so they have to have
grog!' he enthused.

They certainly did. Greg ordered two Crown Lagers
before I could stop him and I ordered two more Bundy
chasers just to make sure the Crown Lager was effectively killed before it entered my lower intestine. The TV
was playing an old football grand final from about ten
years earlier and Greg loved it. But there was something
mind-numbingly perverse about this sportsmen's bar.
Besides the eighteen-years-and-one-day-old barman,

Greg and I were the only other people in the place. There were no other sportsmen. There weren't even any sports-ladies. It was as if people actually came to shopping malls to *shop*. So we asked the eighteen-years-and-one-day-old barman if he knew of any other licensed premises we could drink at in the shopping mall.

'Nuh.' He looked at us like we were on day-release or something.

We sat with the rum chasers and pooled our mental resources. And that's when the barman said, 'What about the bar at the bowling alley?'

Greg thought this was a terrific idea. 'I've never got pissed in bowling shoes before.'

That added to the cost, of course. And the bowling alley was packed full of people bowling. But the bar was, once again, empty. There was no one leaning against it, or near it, or showing any signs of doing so. It seemed weirdly un-Australian.

The shoes cost us a $20 deposit, of which we got $15 back. The bar had Bundy and it was cheaper than the sports bar, too. So we had two doubles. And now we had some confidence. Greg even wanted to bowl. But that would be to lose sight of our mission's main objective – to get trashed in a shopping mall in three hours, before seeing a film with the GFs. If we did this well and if we did this properly, as I said to Greg, then there was the very real chance that we would never be asked to accompany the GFs on a shopping-mall expedition again. Ever. That idea struck a very deep and profound chord in Greg; in fact, it almost seemed to sober him up a little, as if ready to take on further and more powerful drinking.

By now we'd worked out a few more shopping-mall drinking logistics. You could certainly drink at the cinema, at its bar, so that would be the last place we'd head to before meeting the GFs at the box office at 9.15 pm. The barman at the bowling-alley bar, who was now fully and enthusiastically informed of our plan, suggested that the penultimate bar should be the one at the Pancake Parlour, right next to the cinema. 'No one ever drinks there, and I don't reckon I've seen anyone at the bar, ever; but even if you have to sit in one of those little pancake booths and eat a pancake or two, you'll be able to order a drink . . .' This was the sort of barman I liked.

Besides those options, things seemed a little dry, however. 'No, wait!' said Greg. 'The department store. The department store!'

'What about it?'

'It's got a restaurant on the top floor, behind the furniture and electrical section!'

Of course it did. We could drink there with the old grannies and the mums with their prams and the divorced dads enjoying early weekend visiting rights. But the film was still some time away, so we had to be able to fit one more drink in before the restaurant.

'You could always go to the supermarket grog shop and buy a half-bottle of Bundy there. Drink it out by the bus-stop lane, like everyone else does . . .' Once again the barman had come to the rescue. We had one more with him and even tipped.

By the time we got to the box office we were giggling like schoolgirls. I had run Greg through a few worst-case scenarios as we sat in the Pancake Parlour, on our last Bundy before we met up with the GFs. *You've gotta be cool. You've gotta be, like, 'Tan, honestly, Ben and I have just had a couple at the Pancake Parlour cos we were bored and hungry* . . .' But deep down I knew Greg was going to fluff it. Tan was the alpha-male, and she would win.

We walked towards the box office, a little late. I was hoping that the late arrival would see Tan a little flustered and that might distract her – what with having to buy the tickets and all she might not have her eerie third-sense in-built breathalyser turned on.

Everything was going OK until Greg started to laugh. Tan looked at him a second time, just as she was about to buy the tickets. 'Greg!' He laughed more. She said his name once more, intoning it even more scarily than she did first-off. She turned on me. 'This is your fault, isn't it?'

Tan made us sit a few rows in front of her and my GF. 'I'll be watching you both very carefully,' she said as she handed us our tickets. My GF didn't say a thing. In fact, she seemed a little bit sad. She didn't even say anything when we got home later that night – and she usually did. And that was the beginning of the end of that relationship. Which just goes to show how evil shopping malls are and what they can do to a young couple in love.

If this all seems too revolting, and if it has made you feel more than a little less likely to drink cheap rum again, then please remember but one thing. This is the Mr Hyde side of dark spirits. There is the nicer if somewhat morally flawed side, too: Dr Jekyll. And in the world's best whiskies and bourbons and rums we sometimes meet him. It is a captivating, mesmerising experience – even if through it you sometimes catch a glimpse of the doctor's darker depths.

9

There's something about sherry

Some of the finer kinds of sherry are really supernacular.
– George Saintsbury, *Notes on a Cellar-Book*

Not only are some of the finer kinds of sherries super-nacular, but they are also super-effortless. They are not just drinks, but they are a friend, a masseur, an executive assistant, and a quiet yet nonetheless effective conversationalist. Manzanilla, for instance, at about 15 per cent alcohol, and in a half-bottle, is just about the perfect way to prepare dinner, or lunch.

Remove the bottle-top's plastic capsule and stopper (or in the case of an increasing number of good manzanillas, the screw-cap) and pour yourself a small amount of fridge-door-temperature sherry. Get the various dishes underway, and by the time you've got everything in the oven or on the simmer or under the grill a plate of Dead-Things-on-Toast will have appeared – and appeared as miraculously as has the new sense of calm that now envelops you. But wait, there's more. As if by some grand universal design there will now be two glasses of sherry left in the half-bottle for you and Mrs You to all-too-naturally drink. As you polish off the DTOTs the tangy and nutty, pale and dry fortified wine will dissolve what tiny traces of pre-5.30 pm angst might remain in your body. You'll wonder why you don't drink half a bottle of fino or manzanilla every night of the week; and you'll wonder why you've been suffering through full bottles of loudly flavoured *shuddernay* for so many consecutive evenings. Besides, at 13 or 14 per cent alcohol, these chardonnay wines are not that much less powerful than a good, light sherry.

Tangy, nutty, pale and dry. Not creamy, treacly, sweet or brown. The best styles of sherry are more like white wines than they are like bad port. Cream sherries still exist, of course, and they are still relatively inexpensive products with ye olde labels, quite often besporting some sort of duck, usually in flight. I don't know why sweet, cream sherry labels ever need a duck on them. Maybe they were designed to go with the ceramic ducks hanging on the sitting-room wall? The duck on the label could hardly have been an early form of 'serving suggestion' advice. Old aunties and grannies probably didn't like duck anyway – *too stringy and dry*, they'd have no doubt complained. Or *too fatty and smelly*. Old aunties and grannies always had two opposing answers for every conceivable question. And they'd use them interchangeably, just to keep the youngsters on their toes.

Sherry has been a myriad of drinks and tastes over its long and often very troubled history. It's been Falstaff's sack, it's been Auntie Joyce's pale cream. It's been made in Australia from Spain's native palamino grape; it's been made in Germany from distilled potatoes and a few other flavourings. It's been shipped to a fledging settlement in America, and it's been stolen brazenly from a barricaded Cadiz, when Sir Francis Drake 'singed the beard of the King of Spain' back in 1587. Drake made off with 2900 pipes of the stuff. That's about 1.1 million litres of drink. Not a bad snatch-and-grab job. No wonder Drake is so often credited with kick-starting the English love for sherry.

Because the English do love sherry. Or they did. Some of them still use it, as if almost out of tradition; but in many ways good sherry has become something of a rather too solitary interest for members at the sharper end of the wine appreciation business. Wine wankers who know their wine drink pale sherries. Or, at least, I do. But I have to, because I have this thing about drinks that have suffered. Gin. Vermouth. They both suffered and nearly went out of business. I guess I like an underdog; or a nearly extinct dog. If you've still got doubts about drinking a dead-yeast-affected acetaldehydic 15-per-cent-by-volume fortified white wine from Spain's city of Jerez – and drinking it before your dinner – let me explain this drink to you.

Sherry's name comes from its city of birth: Jerez. Or Jerez de la Frontera. Jerez is in Andalucía. And it's near to the other two key sherry towns of Puerto de Santa María and Sanlúcar de Barrameda. Jerez was settled in its first instance – well, at least in terms of commerce – by the ever-cash-register-carrying Phoenicians. Being on the south-west tip of Spain, Jerez was of immediate interest to the Carthaginians and then, naturally enough, to the Romans. They called it Ceritium. That might sound like a brand of laptop computer chip, but it's not. The Romans liked Ceritium, because they expanded its vineyards and winemaking production and drank a lot of the stuff themselves.

Then Jerez got bashed about by the Visigoths and manhandled by the Vandals. Then it was taken over by the Moors (who let the locals continue making wine). The Moors called Jerez *Seris*, which, in terms of etymology, is not too far away from sherry. The Moors set up a good civic infrastructure which the re-conquering Christians preserved. For three hundred years Jerez made white wine that was beginning to morph and oxidise into something not too dissimilar to the sherry we know today. In the sixteenth century the English and the Spanish got cranky and Drake singed the Spanish king's beard. The result – as we have heard – meant that sherry's *sacke* was the drink of England for – one or two minor wars notwithstanding – about 400 years. It even survived the Peninsula Wars of the Napoleonic period, despite the fact that most of the town of Jerez itself didn't. But then things went sour. Phylloxera hit and wiped out huge amounts of vineyard. Phylloxera is a little bug that eats vine roots. Once it takes hold in the vineyard, the vineyard is finished. At the same time sherry was being copied and mimicked and ripped-off all around the world. The price fell out of the sherry game, and the original sherry producers were hardest hit. Stumbling through the early part of the twentieth century it took business consolidation to sort out the unfortunately rickety mum-and-dad nature of the industry. Even in the early 1990s the region was cutting back vineyards in an effort to make demand reconnect with supply. Or the other way around.

But some things show promise, and there's still some fight. As recently as 1996 the word 'sherry' was granted an EU imprimatur. Only those wines from Jerez could use the word. A German potato-spirit copy couldn't. And nor could, from 2007, an Australian dry white fortified wine. It might be made from the palamino grape and it might be made in a solera system but it couldn't use sherry's name. Which is why the Australian wine industry has opted for the name *Australian Dry White Fortified Wine*. Catchy, isn't it? Given I can buy an imported half-bottle of manzanilla from Sanlúcar de Barrameda for about $15, I think I'll stick to the original stuff. Particularly at elevenses.

When you drink pale fino or manzanilla sherry at 11 am you need to be sure you are drinking very fresh stock. Freshly bottled, freshly shipped (in climate-controlled containers), and freshly drunk. At 11 am. No point letting the long and lingering day get in the way of you and a glass of fresh fino, is there?

Fino and manzanilla. The former is the same as the latter, excepting that the latter comes exclusively from a smaller town at the estuary of the Guadalquivir, the aforementioned Sanlúcar de Barrameda. It's about twenty kilometres north-west of Jerez, and just a short drive up the river into the port from a little town called Bonanza. Sanlúcar gets more of the sea breezes than the bodegas in Jerez. It's a little cooler at night and a little more infused with all those flavours from the sea, from the Gulf of Cadiz, and from the Atlantic Ocean, blown into the bodegas by the moist air of the Potente breeze. This means that Sanlúcar's manzanilla sherry has just a touch more tang and a touch more nuttiness about its person, thanks to the thicker layer of flor that grows. Jerez fino is a wonderful thing, that might be true; but the hardcore sherry suckers go to Sanlúcar, and to manzanilla. Even at 11 am.

Don't think for one minute that this sort of drinking is, well, you know, a bad sign. This sort of drinking is not wrong. It doesn't mean you have a problem. People drink coffee at eleven o'clock in the morning. They drink tea at that time, too. They drink soft drink and soy decaf lattes and fruit juice and boost juice and all sorts of bottled water. Sherry is as good if not better a drink than any of those beverages. And there's your key word. Beverage. Sherry, if taken as a small glass of wine at eleven o'clock in the morning, is just another beverage. More importantly, it contains no caffeine, no sugar, no chlorine, no food colourings, no dairy. No soy. And no decaf. It is an entirely tolerant drink, waiting to help you navigate your way through the late morning, on your ultimately inevitable path towards lunch. And because it has that healthful 15 per cent alcohol, it also makes for fewer terse phone calls at midday and a much happier disposition on anyone sitting down to a late 1 pm luncheon.

But how to administer it?

In a small wine glass pour about a half-measure of pale sherry. You might have something close to about 80 or 90 millilitres. Have this wine chilled and drink it in about three or four sips – then order your coffee. Or make your coffee. Yes, this is the sad part of the story. Unless you are in Spain there's a very strong possibility that you'll not have a handy corner bar open at eleven o'clock to naturally and nonchalantly serve you a small glass of fresh, chilled, pale sherry. Sad, like I said; but if you can't change your own society at least you can change *you*. Society might not make eleven o'clock sherry-sipping publicly and politely possible, but you can. In the privacy of your own office. If you work alone.

Of course, if this sounds too anarchic then you've always got the acceptable fallback position of food. In emotionally repressed societies when you are eating food you are occasionally allowed to drink. Sherry doesn't mind this imposition; indeed, it rather likes it. Sherry and a range of foods make for a sort of quiet harmony often missing from the more intricate and gastronomised food and wine matching.

Part of the reason pale sherries are so interested in dining with you is found in their subtle personalities. Fino and manzanilla are both made from a fairly neutral grape – palamino. It's picked quite young to retain as much acidity as possible. The grapes are turned into white wine along the normal routes. When it is fermented a little bit of spirit is added to set the wine at about 15 per cent alcohol by volume. The wine then goes into a barrel or pipe. But the barrels are only filled up about three-quarters full. The empty headspace provides the conditions in which flor yeast can grow – blown about the bodega by the Potente. This yeast grows on the surface of the barrelled sherry, forming a protective layer between the sherry and the air in the barrel's headspace. It's from the flor yeast that the sherry takes its nuttiness and some of its tang – and a little bit of autolysis, or dead-yeast poo smells. Just like in some champagne. Yum.

After two years the pale sherries are transferred into a kind of kindergarten for flor sherries, where they play for a further two years before going into a solera system, which is the be-all and end-all for all flor yeast pale sherries. Stacks of sherry barrels work together, the oldest wines in the barrels on the bottom and the youngest, newest wines at the very top. Each time some of the oldest wine is drawn off for bottling, the next youngest wine is fed into the old boy's partially drained barrel. This repeats all the way up to the top of the solera, guaranteeing not just a complexity and subtlety of flavour, but a good and reliable house-style of sherry. Which is part of the reason good pale sherry is one of the world's most reassuring drinks. We change but it doesn't. And in the hundreds and hundreds of years that it has been around it has picked up some very interesting dining companions. And they are quite often dining companions that a lot of other wines don't much get along with.

Like tomatoes. Pick up any tossy wine and food guide and someone called Sebastian will be telling you that tomato acidity *absolutely destroys* the flavour of *fhine whine*. I'm not going to be told what to do about tomatoes and wine by anyone, whether it be fine wine or not; and I'm not going to be told what to do with that wine by someone called Sebastian. But I am a little counter-suggestible, it's true.

I can happily drink most things with most foods, with the possible exception of cabernet and chocolate; but that's mostly because I don't much like chocolate. Tomatoes and pale sherry do something very special, though. Or, rather, they don't do something special. This is the point I am trying to make about fino and manzanilla when it comes to certain foods. The drink and the dish seem to be a natural combination. So natural that you don't even notice the fact they are married or friends or even at the same party together.

A simple tomato soup can help explain this further.

Finely chop up half a brown onion. Fry it over medium heat along with some olive oil in a stainless-steel pot. Add a few leaves of fresh basil and a finely chopped clove of garlic. Stir it about and then tip in four peeled and chopped tomatoes. Fresh ones. Canned ones are OK, too. Reduce the heat to about one matchstick's worth (or use a diffuser mat) and let this cook for about 45 minutes. Add a cup of chicken or beef stock and then transfer the lot to a vitamiser. Vitamise like merry heck until you get a smooth sort of baby food. Strain this through a sieve into a pot to eliminate the tomato seeds, add another cup of stock, and then gently reheat. Just before you serve it pour a spoonful of sherry into the pot. Stir it about and then ladle into bowls – a dollop of cream at the bottom of each bowl isn't a bad idea.

What is the combined effect of the bowl of soup and the glass (or two) of pale sherry? Conversation. The food and the wine will work modestly together so that you and Mrs You can *talk*.

Manzanilla does a very similar thing to a green prawn. Buy as many green prawns as you dare. (The equation as far as the sherry goes is about six prawns to one half-bottle, per man.) Buy tiny green prawns, the tiniest ones you can find. Into a large pot of boiling salted water drop two bay leaves, one sprig of rosemary and one sprig of thyme. And a pinch of salt and half a lemon, too. Add the prawns and cook them as little as you dare. Drain, refresh them under cold water, and plonk them on a plate with a bowl of mayonnaise and a few more lemons. Pepper is handy. Make sure the sherry is extra cold. And always eat this dish out of doors, with white napery the size of bed sheets.

Gazpacho is a bit of an exception. You don't drink

sherry with gazpacho, you drink it immediately before the gazpacho and immediately after the gazpacho, which sort of turns gazpacho into a drinking game or a three-course liquid luncheon.

Peeled tomatoes, cucumber, garlic, old white bread, and maybe a touch of red pepper get whizzed in the food processor before being mixed with water, salt and pepper. Stir in some sherry vinegar. The next day, before you serve, adjust the consistency (there's no hard and fast rule here – it's a matter of personal taste) and stir through some really good extra virgin olive oil. The key elements are the garlic and the olive oil. Both have to be fresh, the former shouldn't be too pungent and the latter shouldn't be in any way rancid. This is powerful soup, which might explain why it's best to fortify yourself *before* with some sherry, and cleanse yourself *afterwards* with some more . . .

Pale sherries are also – along with good white port – about the only drink that can go punch for punch with olives. Which means you don't have to put the little things in Martinis . . . You can eat them instead.

If this is starting to sound like a way of life you could get used to, the good news is that the pale sherries are but one part of this drink's broader style.

Amontillado. This is one step on from fino, in terms of the beverage's development of flavours and richer complexities. Amontillado starts out life as fino, but it is then removed from the solera system, often because its flor layer refuses to properly form. This wine is drained away from its protective if dysfunctional yeast ceiling and then given a booster shot of spirit, to bring it up to about 17 per cent alcohol. It now goes into a barrel, filled right to the top. The extra alcohol kills off any chance of new yeast growth, and the fullness of the barrel means the wine therein oxidises at a very slow rate. The colour of the wine deepens as it loses its green fino tinge and moves towards a warmer amber hue; the flavours also become enriched; and the smells move from ocean and tang to rancio.

Rancio is possibly one of the world's best wine-tasting terms. It is so imprecise and means so many things, depending on which area of the grog business you are in. Sherry, port, liqueur muscats and tokays, even brandy and cognac. All of them use this term, and all of them use it just a little bit differently. The first thing to remember, though, is to always be fooled by the word's foreign charm. To understand it in English means that you understand the word to mean rancid. *Rancio* is much nicer.

In amontillado sherry, rancio expresses itself through aged barrel flavours; it is a little bit nutty and a little bit, well, like old timber. The key to it is its minimalism. Too much rancio and you've wrecked the soup. You should be *just* able to detect this, what is, in effect, defect. Remember, the *Mona Lisa* is not perfect.

It's no wonder that amontillado sherry suits earthy flavours. Like another one of the world's most humble yet satisfying soups: pumpkin.

Shit a brick. This is becoming a recipe book, but here we go . . .

Chop up enough unpeeled pumpkin to cover a pizza tray. The pieces should be just a bit bigger than a golf ball, but not, of course, necessarily round, or dimpled . . . Sorry. Sit the pieces on the tray skin-side down. This means they don't stick to the tray. Roast in a moderate oven until the pumpkin is easily pierced with a kitchen knife's point. Remove and, using a knife and fork, take off the skins. Chuck them into the compost bin. Put the pumpkin into the blender. Fry some finely chopped onion in butter for a few minutes and add this too, along with a pinch of nutmeg and a cup of chicken or beef stock. Whiz it thoroughly and then transfer to a pot for reheating and viscosity adjustment. Once again, you can add some cream if you like; and you'll need to adjust the seasoning, too. A bowl of this with some thick slices of walnut bread and the word *rancio* suddenly takes on a fabulous Iberian charm.

And it will do the same thing with a number of very untrendy vegetables. Celeriac cubed and given the tomato-soup treatment will love amontillado too. Or Jerusalem artichokes; or eat some French onion soup and apply this style of sherry to yourself while doing so. And if you're soup-intolerant, which so many people seem to be nowadays, split that pizza tray 50/50 with the pumpkin and some similarly sized pieces of cauliflower. Roast with a scant scattering of paprika; cool, add olive oil, salt, lemon. Arranged creatively on what you imagine to be an attractive platter, these bits of vegetable make a terrific pre-prandial, along with the amontillado, of course. If you've got dainty guests, go for a smaller size of golf ball, however. These roasted veggies, along with a handful of chickpeas, become a good side dish, too; but by then you've probably finished all the sherry and are getting stuck into the tempranillo . . .

And when that's gone, you can always finish off the night with a bowl of ice cream for dessert, doused with a glass of oloroso. Or you could have some sherry-infused trifle. Or just have a trifle party all on its own . . .

Oloroso is a good flavour base for whatever trifle recipe you can come across. The sherry style itself is yet another step or two on from amontillado's richer but by no means sweet disposition. Oloroso can be sweetish, but a true one is always as bone dry as its paler relatives. Richness and sweetness – it's important to differentiate between the two. Oloroso's long barrel conditioning brings on darker colour and more raisined and rich flavours. So there is a more luxurious texture, and often a little more alcohol – up to maybe 20 per cent and beyond – but there's not any sweetness. Unless it is added by the winemaker.

The dryer the oloroso, the more of it you can drink; the sweeter the oloroso and the more the children will want it. And the trifle.

A good trifle should be kept very simple. It is no more than a layer of cake, jam, cake, wine, fruits, custard and cream, from bottom to top. In mid-season trifle form I've been known to eat any leftovers at breakfast, with a glass of demi-sec champagne. It's such an effervescent way to start the day. The trifle should always be made in a clear glass bowl, so you can see the geo-trifical layers within; and it is best made the morning before the afternoon on which the sherry party is being held. You could make it the night before, and many people do, but I find that makes the illicit 'leftovers' a bit too decomposed thirty-six hours later . . .

Here's the drill.

Layer matchbox-sized yet thinnish slices of Madeira or sponge cake on the bottom of the bowl. Supermarket cake is fine. Spread three tablespoons of raspberry jam over the top then repeat the cake layer process. Now pour over a cup of oloroso. You can also add a bit of brandy at this stage, too, particularly if you want the kids to go to sleep early. Now layer the berries into the bowl. About two cups' worth. Strawberries, loganberries, raspberries, that sort of thing. Next put in two cups of custard, over which you'll spread 250 grams of slivered almonds. Whip 300 millilitres of cream until it forms little creamy peaks and add this to the bowl. You will of course have saved a few choice berries with which to attractively decorate the top. Put this into the fridge. Ideal for two people and with the remaining 500 millilitres of oloroso . . .

Some people make trifle with stone fruits. That's very good too. Some people drink sweet dessert wine with trifle, like the lush white wine from the Rhone, muscat de Beaumes-de-Venise. I suppose you could, and it is very nice; but I'll stick with the sherry, thanks.

Trifle parties do not only have to contain sherry, of course. A trifle party and a good punch turn empowered professionals into little children.

I'm not sure if punches are on the way back or not – not the birthday kind, but the liquid ones, in big bowls on the sideboard, surrounded by little cups. I do still see a lot of punch-bowl sets in op shops and at junk markets, though, so maybe this large mixed drink is still trapped in the Menzies era, and even earlier times.

Perhaps the more popular recycling mindset will encourage people to punch once more? Because a good punch is often the result of a few good odds and sods, a few leftovers, a few heel-taps. Why eke out one more under-poured and insulting gin and tonic when that little bit of gin can go into a punch bowl? Why hang on to that fag-end of tequila, why not add a touch of vodka? People seem to think of white spirits as being only useful in smart co-tails, but they play two very other useful hands: punch, and stains . . .

Wastrel's Punch is one of my two favourites, the other being a Planter's Punch, but we will get to that in a moment.

The wastrels are not so much the leftover white spirits that make the isotopic power of this drink, but the people that invariably gather to drink it. And so they should. If you've bought your punch-bowl set from the op shop then it is only right that those who subsequently gather around it are people of the most desperate order – like your family and friends.

Pour all the leftover white spirits into a large punch bowl. 'Leftover' as a volumetric term means any bottle of white spirit with less than a quarter of a bottle to go. Tip these into the punch bowl with the juice of one orange and one lemon or one lime. Don't add chunks of fruit, whatever you do, as this only ends up in the punch cups of young ladies who are then socially embarrassed – do I eat the fruit or try to avoid it? Good ice goes in now; large chunks of it. At this stage I invariably add about a third of a bottle of Pimm's. But where to go to from here is a decision you and only you can make. Each Wastrel's Punch is as individual and as ever-changing as a wastrel himself.

You've probably got just enough alcohol, by this stage; but perhaps some vermouth or some sherry wouldn't be a bad idea now. Fresh peaches should only be used if you've got them. White wine or sparkling white wine should only go in as a last resort – to sort out the final volume and general sea-line – you will probably need a bottle or two, depending on the crowd. Some people like putting nutmeg into punches, but no one I knows does that. Frozen cubes of milk are also pretty problematic. Best leave them out. Or not make them in the first place.

Soda is the filler; lemonade should be used sparingly. A touch of angostura bitters is handy, if only to let anyone watching know that you are a serious punch man. Do not add port. Do not add rum, unless it is light rum, of course. Save the dark rum for the Planter's Punch.

Planter's Punch: equal parts dark and white rum should be combined with half parts lime and lemon juice. Add a good dash or two of grenadine – which is a pomegranate cordial. And add a good dash of Triple Sec, which is a Cointreau-like liqueur made from distilled sun-dried orange skins. (This is good gear for Margarita-making, too.) Add just enough ice and just enough mineral water to make the whole thing punch-perfect: not too short, not too long. Float a few thin slices of lime on the surface of the potion, just to show the assembled Planters that you're doing OK and can still wantonly waste limes as a garnish. This is a punch best drunk in a white suit; or at the very least under a white hat or atop white shoes. All three parts of the ensemble are ideal, of course.

Occasionally you'll have a party and occasionally some uninvited guest will bring a bottle of white spirit that is undrinkable. Boris Yeltsin Vodka. Old Mule Tequila. Lady Jane Export Quality Gin. Jamaican Breeze White-Lightning Rum. If you can't use these to make decent drinks, don't think you can hide them in a punch. You'll only end up sicker. But they do serve some reasonable uses. Like lifting stains.

A good punch party usually involves a few good stains. One hears a lot of stain-lifting advice, but it usually involves acting on the spur of the moment, right when the stain has hit the ground. How crass, to clean the house while holding a party.

True, some white wine on a red-wine stain will help dissolve it. True, some mineral or soda water on any drink stain will do similar things; but only some badly distilled white spirit can deal with white shag-pile carpet and Drambuie the next morning. Sponge, dampen, sponge, dampen. It's like magic.

Lifting your own stains has become a bit of a lost domestic art. Indeed, I don't think they teach it in high school any more. The children are too busy with such coursework as psychology, international studies, and film. Traditions and habits of the past disappear daily, it seems; some go unnoticed, a few with a fight. It is with alcoholic beverages as it is with all other things. Lots of drinks have been left behind. Absinthe, purl, mead, shandies . . .

Although, with absinthe, one can sort of understand why it had to take a bit of time off, go to rehab, and come back a more media-friendly person. Wormwood's active hallucinogenic, thujone, sent people on some fairly bad trips. Van Gogh lost an ear as a result. Absinthe is nothing more than a highly flavoured gin. Aniseed is a big part of that flavour – and wormwood. *Artemisia absinthium*. The trouble was, back in the late nineteenth century, the amount of thujone passing into the finished drink from the wormwood infusion was, well, poisonous. And mind-altering. Absinthe was like taking bad gin with an inbuilt bad-attitude pill. Or was it?

Later twentieth-century chemical analysis of absinthe suggests that thujone got a raw deal. Part of the reason absinthe was so despised and then eventually banned by a raft of European countries had more to do with the sort of people that took the stuff. Artists. Parisian artists. Absinthe also had massive amounts of alcohol. Try 70 and 80 per cent . . . And absinthe is green. *La Fée Verte.* The Green Fairy. High alcohol content coupled with a weirdo colloquial name, and used by artists . . . Well, there was one more problem for absinthe's image. The ritual. Absinthe was added to icy water, at a rate of about one-to-four. This was done with a special absinthe spoon. Like pastis, the drink would go all cloudy. To thus cloud the absinthe with water was known as louching. Anyone doing this properly was considered an absintheur . . .

The stuff has got much less thujone in its contemporary manifestation, but still the alcohol and the aniseed. It still looks like dishwashing liquid, and when you add the water it looks like cloudy ammonia. This is why it's best left to the totally hot mixologist to cream their jeans over.

Such bartenders don't seem to be too interested in bringing back to life other historical drinks. Such as purl. This is a warm beer cocktail. Yes, sounds fantastic, doesn't it. Boil some ale and then add some gin. Or vermouth. Perhaps some sugar and some spice. At the end of the seventeenth century this was the dog's balls. Which is why it was often called the Dog's Nose. And they drank it in the morning. No one drinks it any more.

Nor do they go in for mead so much nowadays, despite the fact that it could very well be man's oldest fermented alcohol. Honey, water, yeast. Mead. It's 10,000 years old, going back to the Hindus, who used it in a worshipful and religious capacity. As did the Norse hundreds of years later; as did northern European monks even further on still. Russian peasants at the time of the emancipation celebrated with it. And now it's mostly gone. Nowadays honey is probably more used in aromatherapy than it is in mead making.

Fashion, tastes, production techniques, refrigeration – all of these factors have combined to see these drinks, to varying degrees, slowly disappear. Some survive in protected habitats or drinkers' zoos, where a small number of imbibers strive to keep the species alive. Others have gone like the Dodo.

One endangered species is fighting back, however. Port. Real port.

10

Never sit on a hard chair after drinking port

Port should rarely be served at breakfast ...
– The Savoy Cocktail Book

Portugal sits on the granite edge of Europe, in a prickly cuddle with its once mortal enemy – and half-brother – Spain. Its eyes might nowadays look towards Brussels, but Portugal's heart still stares out to sea. To the Grand Banks off Canada, to Brazil, and into all the ocean that spreads in between. Living off cod and living on rock, Portugal manages to make one of the most perfect and intriguing wines in the world. From the upper reaches of a sharp and deeply etched river valley in the north of the country comes Port – the accidental, 300-year-old child of political and economic expediency coupled with a harsh and often dangerous geography.

The political and economic father came in the form of William III of England. In 1693 he threw another barb at the French in what was the cranky you-said-that-I-said war of trade that invariably accompanies all the real fighting. French wine was hit with heavy tariffs and taxes; it was even banned for a while. This – for a country and a growing number of English wine merchants who had only a few years earlier started to get the new trend of champagne up and running – was something of a bother. They could no longer just slip across the channel. They had to sail all the way around the north-west tip of Spain and into Oporto, Portugal's northern, second capital.

After some failed starts with *vinho verde* the early English wine merchants soon discovered the rough and robust reds of the Douro Valley. Venturing on mule-back over the *Celebrity Survivor*-like mountain tracks (*not*) of the Sierra de Marao, they penetrated into the small villages. (Given the inhospitable nature of the landscape, one wonders both how and *why* they even managed to start bargaining for the red wines.) With deals done, the wine had to be shipped. First it travelled by a tiny flat-bottomed boat called a *barco rabelo* down the often dangerous rapids of the Douro. Then it went on, in bigger ships, to England. Trouble was, by the time this manly red had made the sea voyage back to London, it had started to spoil. Fortification was clearly required, and this is what the merchants started to do – pouring brandy into the barrels before they were shipped off. Heavily textured and tannic – not to mention fairly fiery – this powerful beverage was to port what Neanderthals were to Man.

But who helped the evolutionary step along? The British claim they were the ones to start adding the brandy, not *after* fermentation, but *during* the process, thus arresting the wine's development, making it a little sweeter, which, in turn, helped counterbalance the Douro Valley's red grape's natural tannin astringency and gruff dryness. But the Portuguese reckon they had that technique down pat already, as it was a practice employed in some of the monasteries in the Douro Valley. Monks were making the first ports as altar wines, adding brandy to still-fermenting red wine, so that it might keep longer and better, and be a little sweeter ... This, of course, seems like a bit of an altar-wine anomaly: I've always thought the stuff was supposed to go off quickly and taste either treacly or vinegary – or both – in order to discourage anyone – or any priest – from drinking too much of the stuff.

Inconsistently and irregularly fortified, Douro reds became England's new 'plonk'. Missing their claret, thanks to the trade bans, they had no other choice, however; so slowly plonk became 'Black-Strap' – a kind of bad, alcoholic Barossa shiraz of its day. With the signing of the Methuen Treaty in 1703, Portugal won further trade advantages with England, covering a range of goods and products; in return England got near-exclusivity to the wine, among other things. The French and their allies would be unable to sample the delights of the new Douro reds ... It's hard to tell who was the winner of that one. Probably the Portuguese, at least for a few years.

The shippers and merchants prospered, but it didn't stay very wonderful for very long. As the trade grew and the wine took off, so occurred the rise of a lot of tricked-up Douro red wines. By the 1750s, as it was later commented, 'they wanted the wine to go even beyond the limits with which nature had endowed it, and, when drunk, to be a liquid flame to the spirits, lighted dynamite when burnt, like writing-ink in colour, a Brazil in sweetness, and an India in aroma ...'

How odd that some cycles in wine marketing don't

change . . . And what was I saying about Barossa shiraz before?

With a trade downturn about to hit, shippers that had established warehousing and blending lodges on the southern side of the Douro, just opposite Oporto itself, at Vila Nova de Gaia, petitioned the prime minister of the day, the Marquis de Pombal. This man established the Pombal Line, which marks the upper reaches of the Precambrian schist that, for the Douro's vines, makes the best grapes. This was not the last time the Marquis de Pombal would bring an authoritarian note to port's proceedings. He also set up 'The Company', which was a more colloquial term for *The Companhia Geral da Agricultura das Vinhas do Alto-Douro*. It became Pombal's virtual, personal monopoly; but he did reorganise the port business, from the vineyards down to the lodges, despite the often legitimate grievances of the English shippers and merchants of Vila Nova de Gaia. And he also rebuilt Lisbon after the 1755 earthquake, developing Pombaline buildings, designed to survive future seismic shocks. Half prime minister and half tyrant, he ended up being sacked by the new queen, Maria I, in 1777. She closed down 'The Company' and a disgraced Pombal disappeared from the story of port. And all this while port was still Douro red. It wasn't until the end of the Napleonic Wars that port became Port – a set and determined style of fortified red (and sometimes white) wine.

Although it didn't happen without some degree of resistance. Joseph Forrester (a wine shipper who eventually drowned in the rapids of the Cachao de Valeria when his boat capsized – he headed straight to the bottom thanks to the heavy money belt he was wearing) thought such fortification an adulteration. And this was in the 1840s, when port was strongly entrenched. Forrester thought that Douro red wines were perfectly good as they were – as dry red wines. The growing port industry didn't. But 150 years later some of them do agree. At a time when port's popularity has waxed and waned and at a time when table wine is once again very firmly king, more Douro Valley port producers are releasing Douro Valley table wines. Whites, rosés, and reds. And some of them are superb wines. But they are not port.

I'm not being an historical romantic about this. If I were an historical romantic then I'd also like retsina. I merely qualify my liking of port on the taste of port. Oh, and maybe the Douro Valley, too.

Port makes you think of things long past. The fantasy world of a bygone era raises itself from a strange and murky depth. But only after you've drunk all the port . . .

I did. I stayed up until last and then drank all the remaining port.

The car journey up into the Douro was a long and slow one, because it had snowed, and all of Oporto and its neighbouring residential districts had put the kids in the cars and gone up into the mountains to see the snow. 'Look at all these idiots,' said Miguel, my brand-new travelling companion. He was driving the car and he was a furniture importer. Miguel and his girlfriend, Joana, were taking me up into port country. We were meeting Zarga and Carla and Antonio and Claudia. And we were all staying at Quinta Nova. And we were all doing that because it was a long weekend and because Joana worked for the Quinta. And no one else was there, despite the winter wonderland on the higher roads leading into the Douro.

Joana had taken me over at the Portuguese Wine Exhibition in Oporto. She was one of those pony-tailed, five-foot-nine bossy brunettes against whom no one stands a chance. These sorts of girls – sorry, I mean women – really do dominate the world of wine, behind the scenes . . .

'No, no; it is not a . . . a . . . What word did you say?'

'Imposition.'

'Oh, yes, I know that one! No! You are not *imposing* yourself. We are just a bunch of friends and we are having a weekend away. You must come with us. The Douro is magnificent.'

She went on and on about the Douro, but would always say, 'Ah, but you have been here before, yes, I keep forgetting . . .'

But I'd forgotten. I'd forgotten how mind-stoppingly panoramic the Douro is. The wide arch of the river valley, the shades of meaning that seem to rest in the partially shaded curves of the valley walls; the black-green flow of the Douro itself, nowadays tamed by a series of five dams, preventing it from its old winter outbursts and summertime trickles.

On each side of the river perched vineyards of various design. Some were the *socalcos* set-ups, going back to Roman times and earlier. There were the terraced vine-yards contouring along the side of the slope, each row making a big, landscaped step, with a stone wall behind it and a stone wall in front of it, falling down to the terrace below. Then there were the newer *socalcos*, with an eye for economy. Rather than one landscaped step per row of vines, maybe eight rows of vines would share one larger, if not-so-gently-sloping step. Other, rougher-looking terraces were *Patamares*; these were simply steps carved out of the land, with no stone supporting them from either in front or behind. Two rows of vine per step, and a healthy layer of weeds and other companion cover crops to prevent too much deadly erosion. And then, on the higher reaches of the slopes, there were the *Vinha ao Alto* vineyards, where trellising helped the vines keep in some sort of collective unison, despite the dizzying heights and the wind and the sparse soil.

The Douro Valley was the first wine area in the world to classify itself. Vineyards get an old-fashioned sort of school grade, from A to F. Twelve factors are all individually scored to come up with this grade, and in each factor a vineyard can get positive or negative scores. The maximum score a perfect vineyard might achieve is 1680 points, which is 480 more than it needs to be classified A. The minimum score is *minus* 3430, which would be a pretty shitty vineyard indeed, as anything below 400 points is an F vineyard. Each grade is 200 points apart. Quite a system. I bet the adjudicators are popular people . . .

The twelve factors of judgement run the gauntlet of the obvious to the highly interpretable. Altitude, productivity, nature of the land, locality, vine training, grape varieties, slope, aspect, density of planting, soil and degrees of stoniness, vine age, shelter . . .

This makes the finished product's classification system look dead easy. Group One port is port you can raise a mortgage on. True. Group Two is port fit for treatment. And Group Three is port that usually ends up as a distillation. Most port is Group One, of course. And the best stuff comes from the best sites, with the best soil.

Then again, it's not really soil up here, in the Douro,

it's that schist – the sort of stone that looks like it could make a very good billiard table. It splits vertically, and almost perfectly straight. And it maintains its structural integrity. Which is why the vignerons of the Douro use it to make strainer posts for the vineyards. This schist is so strong it can be fashioned into a garden stake, as strong – or nearly – as steel. Schist was Pombal's concern. Wherever it ran out, towards the top of any section of sloping river valley, was the mark of the Pombal Line.

Between 1758 and 1761 Pombal's Boundary Commissioners traipsed all up and down the asthma-inducing heights of the Duoro, their work setting up 335 granite markers, carved with the date of establishment, and the word FEITORIA. It means factory in Portuguese, so it means where you can stop making the wine in the Douro . . .

About 100 feitoria survive today, and there was one way above the winery and other buildings at Quinta Nova. It lay beyond a stone-lined orange orchard and almond grove, facing the south, and capturing all the sun, like some sort of reverse alluvial gold sluice. It had high schist-built dry walls, and a strange symmetry, despite the fact it wasn't entirely symmetrical. Each pocket of the grove contained two or three orange trees, and, higher up, three or four almond trees. From the same non-soil that produced the Douro's best port grapes – Touriga Naçional, Tinta Barroca, Tinta Cão, Touriga Francesa – came bittersweet oranges and almost perfect almonds. And subsequently the orange juice that I drank in the morning, and the lightly roasted almonds without the faintest trace of rancidity that I ate every evening with my long drink: white port, tonic, and a twist of lemon. A plate of almonds was reason and conviction enough for me to drink most of the bottle this way. Even Joana and her friends were a bit surprised . . .

It was another 100 or so metres above the grove and closer to the sun that I found the feitoria. It was a large granite marker about the size of a small wrestler. The two top lines read FEIT and then ORIA. Below this, and sloping from left to right, as if carved by a tiring stone-mason, was the date 1758.

The soil around it was still the non-soil schist, although now it was browner, and more broken down, and parts of it even seemed muddy. Above the feitoria, some five or ten metres higher, the layer of schist had lost its personality, and it was thinner. It was as if the further the schist was from the river's edge, the less of a calling it had for the port at the end of the river's journey. Which is why a lot of this land was now being planted with those Douro grape varieties that might yet become the table wines of tomorrow. It was cheaper land, too.

Descending the slope was harder than climbing up it, such was the nature of the ground underfoot. But it did give me a thirst.

Back in the Quinta, my new Portuguese friends had taken the afternoon off, to sleep. The middle-aged couple that ran the Quinta and roasted the almonds and squeezed the orange juice and cooked the multiple soup, meat and rice dishes for lunch and dinner every day had also observed a long afternoon break. Which left an Australian to get up to some educational benchmarking, calibration and mischief. The Quinta Nova had a good stock of port, in its many guises. It was time to do a tasting.

I started with my other best new friend, white port. White port divides the port-drinking community. Por-tuguese port people like it because it is not red, and you can drink it as an apéritif. It also adds another layer of interest to the whole port story. Serious port connoisseurs don't like it because they think it's always too sweet, always without much character, and, in the words of Ernest Cockburn, 'the first duty of port is to be red'. White port has little if any skin maceration, and is aged for a relatively short time by port standards. Maybe eighteen months. Those connoisseurs reckon there's no need to bother with white port while you can still buy manzanilla; but I'd never dream of mixing manzanilla with tonic and a twist of lemon zest . . .

The most important thing about white port is that it puts you in the mood.

Next stop is ruby port. This is a basic, and perhaps quite an original port, given two or three years' maturation and then sold as a light, fruity fortified wine. People used to mix this sort of thing with lemonade. That's about all I thought you could do to it to make it more interesting. Ruby port, when it is good ruby port, is not a bad way to get children into the whole game.

Tawny port is where things become more serious. The basic stuff is aged anywhere between two and five years in cask, and is really not that much more fascinating than ruby. Aged tawnies are more like it, however. With six or more years of cask rest under their belts, they can often be released as ten-, twenty- or even forty-year-olds. There's some young and some much older material in these wines; the age mentioned on the label is only the average age.

Some of the best ports of all are those tawnies known as *colheitas*. These are vintage wines that are often twenty or more years old, and they are not bottled from cask until the shipper reckons them to be ready. They are often topped up a little with some fresher port as they rest in cask, but otherwise these are wines straight out of a time capsule.

More confusing still is LBVP. Late Bottled Vintage Port. This is port from a vintage year that's considered not quite up to a true vintage classification. It's held in cask for longer than a vintage port – maybe four, five or six years – and then bottled off. These, like all of the wines already mentioned, are wines that do not require any more time in the bottle. They are not wines for cellaring. They are designed to be drunk now, or at least pretty soon. Which is why I didn't feel too bad about opening so many different bottles of port in Quinta Nova . . .

The grand poo-bar of all port is, of course, vintage port. This is the best imaginable ruby port of all time, from the best vineyards and best years and best casks. Bottled two years after the vintage date, it is designed to spend many years in cool cellars, resting, going into deep hibernation, before after, say, twenty years or so, it's ready to be decanted and drunk. Vintage port isn't ready, they reckon, until it has 'cracked'. That is, until the tannins in the wine have all fallen out of the solution, leaving that thick deposit on the bottom side of the resting bottle, and until the spirit and the cask-oak tannins and the fruit flavours of all those Douro grapes have integrated and harmonised. That's when a vintage port is ready to be opened.

And to do that you need some port tongs.

Lugging a pair of steel and timber port tongs back with your check-in luggage, through three international airports and one very bossy domestic one, you get a lot of funny questions and experience a lot of annoying delays. In x-ray machines they must look like some sort of dangerous weapon. In a way, they are. But only to the person silly enough to operate them.

Port tongs are about two feet long. They've got wooden, insulating handles and they work like any other pair of tongs do. Sort of. The sharp end of a pair of port tongs has two enclosing, round, clasping grips. The idea it that the final rounded grip will fit very snugly around the neck of a bottle of port. No, this is not how you drink from the bottle.

Heating the port tongs up in a fire, until they are white hot, you then use them to grasp the port bottle's neck. Remove the port tongs, then immediately, and with some courage, grasp the whole area with a very thick and very damp cold cloth. The sudden change in temperature means, what with a careful click of your wrist, the top of the bottle snaps cleanly off, at a point just below the bottom of the cork. If, like me, you had an old bottle of 1970 Fonseca and you wanted to be sure that none of the old and possibly fragile cork would disintegrate under the effects of a corkscrew, then this tried and trusted – not to mention very traditional and silly – way of opening a bottle of port would work perfectly.

Maybe it was the drinks we'd had before we got to the port that were the problem. Maybe heating up a pair of port tongs on a gas cooker is not the ideal way to break them in. Maybe I just needed more practice. But that will have to wait until the next trip to Portugal. The 1970 Fonseca bottle remained intact; the tip of one end of one arm of the port tongs snapped off. Which makes you wonder just how much of any drink's grand and rich tradition, how much of its rich tapestry of anecdotes, and how many of its great characters are embellished and imbued with something of a drinker's lively imagination?

Via a corkscrew, the cork came out a little crumbly, but that's what wine sieves and decanters are for. The old 1970 Fonseca was with us in all its shape and structure and beautifully spirituous fruit for about half an hour. And then it was gone; not physically, but metaphorically. Some of the wine remained in the bottom of the decanter, but the life that was in the wine had been released like a genie in a bottle. It gave us three wishes and left. Which makes you feel all happy and all sad, and all at the same time.

Afterword

What is there left to do, but to drink and watch the view?
– Mental as Anything, 'Too Many Times'

Winter storms give way to spring; but has this drinker learned anything? I have always drunk solidly: never moderately, never apologetically, always to my professional detriment (and cost), and never have I been a hypocrite. I drink.

'What do you do, Ben? It's just that your name sounds familiar . . .' A receptionist at a newspaper I work for asked me this very question just the other day.

'I drink,' I replied.

'Oh, yes, that's right; you're one of our contributors. I'll just put you through. Ha, ha.'

I'm a juicer, as Janis Joplin said. I'm not a water man. I'm neither a social drinker nor a binge drinker; I'm not an occasional drinker or a wine connoisseur; I do not like the odd drop, I don't enjoy a beer after work. I'm never up for one or two and I don't exasperatingly explain that I might be able to fit a quick one in. I drink. Whenever I can get my hands on it. And if anyone has a problem with that, well, I think they know what they can go and do.

But have I learned anything?

For every 10,000 drinkers there are 10,001 disasters. But that doesn't matter because drinkers cannot count. They have seven beers at the pub before getting home late and yet always manage to say *they've only had a couple*. I blame school maths teachers for this problem.

No matter how many drinks you've had at any one or any multiple sittings, you always need one more. No one – not even a maths teacher – is to blame for this phenomenon. It is an example of the ever-illuminated and optimistic spirit of human nature. And why we still, as a race, cannot explain the notion of Time. Speaking of which . . .

Drinking regularly at lunchtime helps the rest of the day take shape. This is a wonderful truism. Most people in the afternoon do exactly what they did in the morning. If they drank a glass of wine at lunchtime then this would not be the case, and we would have a greater diversity of mind and thought in what nowadays passes for society. Apollonian ante meridians would give way to Dionysian post meridians. Structured mornings would become free afternoons. Evening traffic would be fairly chaotic, however.

Being afraid of drinking or afraid of opening a bottle or being afraid of saying, 'Oh, yes please, I will have another drink!' is a more absurd and dysfunctional form of humanity than that form expressed by the worst drunk. Both behaviours are extremes. The drunk has an excuse – drink – but what excuse does the 'no thanks' non-drinker have? Only non-drinkers discuss the evils of drink.

Alcohol aids appetite and weight gain. Apparently this is a problem. Heavy drinkers are best, then, to take regular exercise. Which gives you a thirst. Go for a swim and then drink like a fish. The only thing to remember is to never break the cycle. It's about maintaining a steady and consistent supply. Motor mowers understand this . . .

Motor mowers. The human body is not that much more sophisticated a piece of machinery than the two-stroke motor mower. Motor mowers either start or determinedly don't start. The problem usually lies with the fuel. Never change the fuel mixture on a motor mower. Never adjust the fuel mixture on a human being. Otherwise you might not start tomorrow morning.

These are all things I have learned; and all have been burned into my brain. They are the only things I know with any confidence. As with the following:

Great hangover remedies: Sex, showers, mineral water, a Bloody Mary – although not necessarily in that order. One of these remedies can work fine just by itself. The whole lot always leads to a repeat of the night before.

Great aperitifs: Campari. Martini. (Gin and tonics are not aperitifs – they are in-between drinks used for whatever occasion or non-occasion in which you require refreshment.) Martinis are the only way to go if you need to do any of the following at or around about 7 pm: greet guests; make a speech; meet your daughter's lesbian lover; cook dinner; go out for dinner; feed the cat; put out the bins; empty the compost; avoid answering the telephone. Of course, as an aperitif, champagne is also perfect; but it does not count – at least as liquor. It may be delicious, it may, via its bubbles of carbon dioxide, transport alcohol so much more efficiently into your bloodstream, but it has no real or measurable alcoholic reckoning value. As I said: it does not count. But that's only when it is properly CHAMPAGNE. No one I know drinks sparkling white wine, whatever that is. *Forgetaboutit.* You either drink champagne or, well, commit suicide. Sparkling white wine ... No, I am not even going to bother to finish that sentence.

Great party starters: Tequila shots. On an empty stomach, before any silly food or wine or drugs are taken, tequila is, well, *like a drug* ... Tequila works best on Friday nights. Or Monday nights.

Great wines: There are no such things. Occasionally you come across a great bottle. Wine, however – being more like food than drink – does let you play favourites. The greatest white wine in the world is chardonnay, but only when it sounds or smells or tastes like chablis. The greatest red wine in the world is pinot noir, but only when it reminds you – on its own terms – of pinot noir. Too much pinot noir is just red wine. This is a sign that God has still not quite forgiven us. Wine and God are more closely linked than any of us care to consider. How irreligious.

Great devivifiers: Nothing devivifies like a brandy and soda. A big glass, too much ice, far too much brandy, and then – if at all volumetrically possible – fit a bit of soda in there too.

Great revivifying devivifiers: Whisky. Scotch single malt; I can take Irish whisky at a pinch. I'll leave Canadian whisky for the Canadians; ditto Japanese whisky. Bourbon, rye and Tennessee – in their best guises – are all drinks I can admire; but they don't revivify my oft-devivified condition. Single malt of your choice, poured with care and drunk with an unread book in quietude only disturbed by the half-sound of a whisky sip is akin to Father Time calling an end to the irksome day's woes, leaving you to fall asleep in the armchair, to half-fight another day.

Beer for drinking: Whatever fresh, local lager you can get, and drunk as cold as you can get it. Preferably move it from the fridge to the ice chest – or, better still, to an ice bucket that's 50/50 ice and water – about ten minutes before you take the top off. Then drink a minimum of six.

Beer for admiring: Ale. Fully developed human males drink one small glass bottle of ale for every six small glass bottles of lager. Ale is food; lager is beer. Ale also lends itself to this low-volume admiration thanks to the fact that it is best appreciated in a beer glass. Or even a wine glass. Seriously.

Good spirits: These are the white ones. Vodka and gin are always neck and neck across my finishing line; buy the best ones your budget will allow, or perhaps even not allow. Keep them in the freezer, excepting your Martini gin, which will be different from your G&T gin, and which will live in the refrigerator. Yes, it can become quite complex, all this drinking. Plymouth gin is *the* gin, but only because gin aficionados are pretentious. Good, high-quality vodka can come from any number of distillers; vodka is not pretentious – but you do pay for what you get.

Bad spirits: Anything you drank when you were eighteen.

Evil spirits: Anything you drank when you were nineteen.

Wrong, just plain wrong: As mentioned earlier, Kahlúa, Tia Maria, Baileys Irish Cream, Cynar, Galliano,

Malibu, Midori, Southern disComfort, and retsina – any kind of retsina. And 99 per cent of home-brewed beer. All of these drinks are just like New Year's Eve – they are entirely for children and idiots. Morally more dangerous are pre-mixed cans and bottles of spirit and soft drink. Bourbon and cola in a 375 millilitre convenience package. How convenient. Drinking them at a party is like going to a restaurant and then opening your own can of bolognese sauce, before eating it directly from said can with your fingers.

One final comment.

People who, on an everyday basis, do not treat wine as no more or no less than food, and people who do not think white spirits are an essential ingredient in a pre-dinner co-tail, NEED TO GROW UP. And now I think it's time to go to the bar. Because I think it speaks to me.